STATE WITHIN LIGHT

STATE WITHIN LIGHT

The Path to Enlightenment

Keith Crossley

Spiritual Mastery

Copyright © 2025 Keith Crossley. All rights reserved.

Copyright © 2025 Keith Crossley

All rights reserved.

This book or any portion thereof may not be reproduced or used in any manner whatsoever without the express written permission of the publisher except for the use of brief quotations in a book review.

Printed in the United States.

ISBN: 979-8-9925017-0-4, ebook
ISBN: 979-8-9925017-1-1, paperback
ISBN: 979-8-9925017-2-8, hardcover

Life provides you with just the right amount of suffering to wake you up spiritually. From that point, it's only a matter of time before you transcend suffering altogether.

-Keith Crossley

CONTENTS

Introduction: Enlightenment is for Everyone 1

Chapter 1: What is Enlightenment? 9

Chapter 2: Lose Yourself to Find Yourself 27

Chapter 3: The Foundation Built on Sand 49

Chapter 4: The Way Forward is Through 73

Chapter 5: How to Transcend the Ego 95

Chapter 6: Revealing Your True Self 117

Chapter 7: Finding the Balance 135

Chapter 8: The Highest Frequency is Love 155

Chapter 9: Self-Actualization 175

Chapter 10: Living in the Light 193

INTRODUCTION

ENLIGHTENMENT IS FOR EVERYONE

Spiritual awakenings often look like mental breakdowns, but I didn't know that when it happened to me. I became a millionaire at the age of 31. I built a small business empire with eight restaurants and over a hundred employees—I lost it all by 36. My mental breakdown happened around 11pm on December 21st, 2017.

When there's not enough money to go around for one company, the stress of making payroll, paying vendors, and even keeping the lights on is brutal. During the previous year, several of my businesses were failing simultaneously, and nothing I did seemed to help. I hadn't slept well in months. My anxiety was through the roof. I felt like I was slowly watching my financial freedom, livelihood, and sense of Self slipping through my fingers. Little did I know, this was only the beginning. I'm not sure how long it had been since I'd cried, but I couldn't suppress my tears that night if I tried. I curled into the fetal position and sobbed, a grown man finally beaten into submission. All the pressure, fear, anxiety, and uncertainty hit at once, like a tidal wave of emotions that swallowed me whole. Agony is the word that comes to mind.

I wasn't just failing at business. I was failing. Worse, I was a failure, and everything I thought I knew about myself clearly wasn't true anymore. How would my family survive? What will my family and friends think? What does this mean about who I am? When the pain felt almost unbearable, something strange happened. For a brief moment, I could sense a part of me that didn't feel any embarrassment, fear, or pain. It was like I was observing myself in agony. I was crying but also watching myself cry at the same time. This wasn't an out-of-body experience; something more akin to awareness or a sense of objectivity. Regardless, whoever was watching was completely at peace and somehow insulated from the suffering.

Although I didn't know it, this was my spiritual awakening, a seemingly unimportant event that would have gone largely unnoticed had I not explored it further. Coincidentally, I watched a documentary earlier that evening that showed a group of people meditating. From a wiser source than intellect, I knew that if there was any chance of me surviving, I'd have to find that peaceful place inside me again.

I tried my first meditation the next morning without any prior experience. Five minutes seemed like an eternity. This was another level of torture because I was alone with the voice in my head. I made it ten minutes on day two with similar results. On day three I went fifteen minutes and continued increasing the time each day. My thoughts were still tormenting me, but every now and then I would experience brief moments of stillness. I craved the stillness. It felt like freedom from myself. Within a few weeks, I was meditating for several hours a day, sometimes waking up at 3 a.m. Truthfully it was a form of survival or escape.

Nevertheless, I noticed that I was becoming less reactive to the voice in my head. My problems weren't going away, but my inner state was noticeably calmer. I remember sitting on my front porch one evening when the reality of my situation hit me. Even if I closed my failing businesses, the pain wouldn't stop. Each location was tied to a ten-year lease, and I was a personal guarantor. It would take years to unwind the financial and legal mess I'd made. If finding inner peace was dependent on my problems going away, I would suffer for the foreseeable future. Out of necessity, I asked myself questions I'd never thought of before. How much control do I have over my thoughts and feelings? Is it possible to be at peace even if my life is a disaster?

My plan was to meditate every morning and evening, and retreat to stillness anytime I felt stressed, anxious, or overwhelmed during the day. I'd have short breaks here and there, sometimes meditating in my car for five or ten minutes. I skipped lunch or got my work done quickly to carve out more time. I meditated every free moment I had—it didn't take long for stillness to become my safe haven.

About eight weeks in I was doing a longer meditation when something miraculous happened. My thoughts completely stopped. I was alone in stillness, simply aware that I was aware. The darkness and silence were beautiful and serene. For the first time in my life, I understood what people meant by inner peace, but I wasn't thinking about it. I experienced it for myself. Suddenly, it felt like I was being pulled forward into a corridor at the speed of light. It happened so quickly that I didn't have time to question or stop it. In an instant, everything I knew about myself and this reality disappeared.

I was immediately absorbed into the most radiant, bright light I could imagine. It was more than just light though. It was energy. No, it was more than energy. It was the energy of love, but a love so far beyond anything I'd experienced as a human that the word love seemed trivial. Light was somehow all around me and running through me at the same time. There was no separation. I was one with God. I don't know how long I spent in the light, but I could have stayed there for the rest of eternity and never looked back.

To say I went into that meditation one way and came out another would be an understatement. Everything was different. My wife and children looked like angels, as if I could see their souls. The trees and grass were alive. I'd stare at a leaf or an ant with childlike wonder as every cell in my body burst with supernatural energy. Fear was replaced with joy. Stress turned into bliss. Judgment became compassion. I loved everyone unconditionally, including myself. Although I'd been deeply religious my entire life, I could not see spirituality the same way.

Whatever light I touched or whatever light touched me was the truth.

The next year of my life was a bizarre contradiction. While my external world collapsed in dramatic fashion, my soul was flying in rarefied air. One business caught on fire. Another flooded. Another was robbed. I had to close four businesses in a single day, fire dozens of good people who didn't deserve it, and face multimillion-dollar lawsuits from angry landlords who rightfully wanted to be paid. Financial ruin shortly followed. By any worldly standard, I should have been a mental and emotional wreck, yet this was the best year of my life. I was walking on a cloud, not out of apathy or indifference, but my inner state was so blissful that I could fully engage with every part of my life without suffering. I was free.

In truth, I didn't really know what had happened to me. Frankly, I didn't care because I felt so good. However, after a year in pure ecstasy, I felt myself slowly drifting further away from this magical state. I spent the next several years chasing that original experience, never quite able to get back to the light. In some ways, my supernatural experience was a blessing and a curse. On one hand I knew what was possible, but on the other I had no idea how to maintain it. I was on a relentless spiritual quest, determined to find the truth again. But this time I had to earn my stripes and there were no shortcuts. If this transcendent state was to become my permanent state, I'd have to learn it, understand it, and become it.

State Within Light is the guidebook I wish I had as I made my spiritual ascent. Although you will not find personal stories from my spiritual journey, this book is a reflection of my process. Truthfully, my story is not what is important. Yours is. Your spiritual journey will not look exactly like mine or anyone else's. Even so, spiritual processes and principles are timeless and universal. The path to enlightenment has predictable signposts and milestones, as well as a final destination that can be described, but must ultimately be experienced.

If someone told me that one day I would write a book about enlightenment, I would have laughed. Then I would have sincerely asked, what is enlightenment? This wasn't on my radar. With that said, I knew from a young age that I would write and speak one day. Call it intuition that straddles the line between personal desire and a spiritual calling. I just never knew what the topic would be. The Buddha said enlightenment is the end of suffering. Well, I do know a little bit about suffering. I also know what it takes to not suffer. The state of enlightenment is not magic or hyperbole. It's a spiritual skill that you learn and practice until it becomes your permanent state. My goal is to make enlightenment accessible to the masses. More importantly, my goal is to make enlightenment attainable for you.

-Keith Crossley

CHAPTER ONE

WHAT IS ENLIGHTENMENT?

> Ethereal: extremely delicate and light in a way that seems too perfect for this world.

Enlightenment is the highest state a human being can attain. It's the ultimate paradox. The more you chase it, the more it eludes you. The more you surrender, the more it finds you. It's not what you think it is, yet everything you already knew it was. It's as confusing as it is profound, as simple as it is complex. Enlightenment is everything and nothing, everyone and no one, the beginning and the end.

If you are confused, good. You've learned your first lesson about enlightenment. You'll never experience it by trying to understand it. Enlightenment is one of the most elusive, mysterious concepts on the planet. Intuitively, you know it's a higher spiritual state that would free you from suffering, but it seems too esoteric, a state reserved for special people who renounce the world, shave their heads, and move to a monastery. Who are you to think that you are capable of enlightenment?

It is true that enlightenment is beyond what the human mind can imagine or comprehend, but that's also the point. It's not about knowing more. In fact, it's about knowing less. The path to enlightenment is largely a process of letting go of what you think you know and who you think you are. You must first empty the vessel so it can be filled by an intelligence far superior to the human mind.

Sometimes enlightenment happens in a single moment, like catching lightning in a bottle. You instantly break through the limitations of your mind, never to be the same. You see your true Self clearly for the first time. You see reality as it is. You pierce the veil and dance with divinity. By transcending this world, you break free from its mental and emotional chains. Other times, enlightenment is a slow process, like building a spiritual foundation one brick at a time.

The Buddha is the most famous archetype for enlightenment, but it's important to remember that he was not always The Buddha. He was a man named Siddhartha, who didn't begin his spiritual journey until age 29. He experienced enlightenment around age 35. For six years, he never found what he was looking for, nor did he fully know what he was looking for. How could he? He had never experienced enlightenment. Then suddenly, after meditating for 49 days under the Bodhi tree, it happened. On day 48, he was just Siddhartha, an unenlightened human being. On day 49, he became the awakened one, The Buddha.

Enlightenment is often associated with a supernatural experience that changes everything. This mythology is one reason why enlightenment seems out of reach for most people. Since they've never experienced anything resembling that level of transcendence, they assume it will never happen to them or they chase an experience believing it will be the end all, be all.

Interestingly enough, the Buddha didn't encourage his followers to seek enlightenment through mystical experiences. He simply said enlightenment was the end of suffering. It's a strange decision considering what happened to him under the Bodhi tree. Why would the Buddha reduce enlightenment to the end of suffering when he personally experienced something that defied reality as he knew it? Clearly the Buddha came to a different conclusion about his experience that day. As miraculous and supernatural as it was, it wasn't the end all, be all. When the experience was over, his consciousness came right back to earth—he was still human. There's only one reason you would not tell your followers to chase a supernatural experience. A supernatural experience is not enlightenment. Don't misunderstand. Supernatural experiences are real, and they can be life altering. Seek long enough and you'll experience things most people cannot comprehend. However, if you chase or cling to these experiences, you've mistaken an enlightening experience as enlightenment.

After his experience under the Bodhi tree, the Buddha initially had reservations about teaching what he learned. However, he eventually distilled his message into something far less sensational than out-of-body experiences in other realms. Instead, he spent the rest of his life teaching about the nature of suffering and how to transcend it. Perhaps his intention in making it so simple was to shield humanity from truths they are not ready for. Maybe he didn't want people to chase after experiences that might not happen. Although there is probably merit to these notions, it's more likely that the Buddha realized that ending suffering is the greatest truth humanity could ever discover. The mere possibility seems tantamount to finding the holy grail or the fountain of youth.

Of course, enlightenment is the end of suffering, but how does it actually work? Once you are enlightened, will life magically bend to your will, and you'll never experience pain, trials, or tragedy again? Will you get a free pass while the universe conspires against everyone who is not enlightened? The Buddha was not naïve, and neither are you. The nature of reality is not going to change, which means enlightenment must be an inside job. Something about the way you think, feel, and interact with reality must change if you want to break free. In that regard, enlightenment must be a choice that is within your control. Many people have successfully learned how to end their suffering. The relevant question is: do you believe it's possible for you?

There is a tendency to deify spiritual masters who lived hundreds or thousands of years ago. They've been elevated to icons or symbols, even idols in some cases. When spiritual masters are put on a superhuman pedestal, it gives humanity an ideal to shoot for, but it also makes the path to enlightenment seem impossible. This is not what the Buddha or any enlightened person would want you to feel. The Buddha said, "I am a finger pointing to the moon. Don't look at me. Look at the moon."

This is a caution to spiritual seekers who look for enlightenment in the wrong place. Religions, scriptures, belief systems, and true spiritual teachers are all trying to point you toward one universal truth. But they are the finger pointing to the moon, not the moon itself. Jesus said it like this. "No man is a prophet in his own country." When you know someone well, you see their humanness, and they don't seem particularly special.

Conversely, when you see someone from a distance, you don't see their humanness. They become an ideal, like a spiritual celebrity who seems larger than life. Rest assured, they put on their pants or robes the same way you do. Viewing them as human doesn't diminish their greatness. It gives you inspiration that if you follow Jesus, you are saved. By following the Buddha, you become the awakened one. If these spiritual masters didn't think enlightenment was possible for you, they would not have shown you the path.

In one sense, enlightenment can be viewed as a process of learning, practicing, and mastering new skills until you crack the code on suffering. The Buddha's core message seems very practical and accessible, and indeed, it is. At first glance, his teachings about the end of suffering could even seem devoid of spirituality in some ways, like he was merely creating a pragmatic formula for life. But it wouldn't be fair to dismiss or discount what happened to the Buddha on day 49. Something was clearly different about that experience than any other he had before.

The genius in the Buddha's approach is he knew that along your path to transcend suffering, you would inevitably discover true spirituality. Transcending suffering is only possible by coming to know the part of you that is immune to suffering, which is your spirit. From there, the spiritual discovery expands to God, the nature of reality, the purpose of life, and much more. In other words, enlightenment is both practical and deeply spiritual.

The everyday experience of being enlightened is to transcend this world in a practical sense. End your suffering here and now. Day 49 is to transcend this world in a supernatural sense, having gone beyond the veil of this reality. Think of it as download to your soul while your brain blows a fuse. You are connected straight to the Source. This Source enlightens you to the unmistakable truth of who you are, the nature of God and the universe, and the highest energy that fuels it all. You do not enlighten yourself. You are enlightened.

The Chinese prophet, Lao Tzu, wrote, "the Tao that can be told is not the eternal Tao." The word Tao means way or path. This verse could be interpreted as "the path that can be described is not the eternal path." Enlightenment is an experience and state of being that is beyond intellect, form, time, and space.

The moment you describe enlightenment as a spiritual concept and put it into words, you reduce it to an intellectual construct. In other words, if you think about enlightenment, you're one step removed from it. Furthermore, if you tell someone about enlightenment, you're telling them what you think about it, and then you're two steps removed from it. It's still a finger pointing to the moon.

This book is also nothing more than a finger pointing to the moon. If you understand the principles and concepts with your mind, you'll acquire more knowledge and amass the vocabulary to regurgitate spiritual truths. However, if you never experience enlightenment for yourself, reading this book will be an intellectual exercise masquerading as spiritual progress. You do not reach enlightenment with the mind. You reach enlightenment by transcending it. This is a spiritual journey only you can take.

The word enlightenment begins with the prefix "en," which means within. Light means light. "Ment" is a suffix that means a resulting state. Enlightenment, then, is a state within light. That's it. And, that is everything. To understand enlightenment, at least intellectually, you need to understand the nature of light.

Light is the most powerful energy in the universe. In fact, it is the electromagnetic energy behind all universes. Only in the last few decades has science been able to detect light that predates stars, atoms, and every other form of matter. Think of it as source energy that makes up three-dimensional reality. In 2019, the Hubble Telescope captured the biggest explosion of light ever recorded. It was a burst of Gamma rays, which are a trillion times more powerful than visible light. This gamma explosion emitted more energy in a few seconds than our sun will emit over ten billion years.

The human brain also runs on electromagnetic energy. An EEG brain scan measures energy moving in the brain at different frequencies and wavelengths. This energy is what you know as brainwaves. For many years scientists thought there were four brainwave states: Delta, Theta, Alpha, and Beta, respectively. Beta was the fastest, most energetic brain wave at the time. It's the state you're in most of the day; you're probably in Beta right now as you read.

When EEG technology improved, scientists discovered an even faster brainwave called Gamma. Gamma brainwaves are different from gamma rays, but they share the same name because they both represent the highest energetic frequencies. Gamma brainwaves are associated with peak cognitive or physical performance, the integration of high-level information, coherent thinking, and flow states. Gamma is also associated with high levels of altruism, compassion, love, happiness, contentment, spiritual understanding, and a sense of oneness. Can you guess which practice generates significantly more gamma brainwaves than other mental exercises? If you guessed meditation, you're right.

The most profound mystical, transcendent, and enlightening experiences often happen when gamma brainwaves skyrocket during practices like meditation. This is a scientific and spiritual transcendence from your normal state to a higher state. You move beyond the analytical mind and immerse your consciousness in more energy and light, i.e., enlightenment. Is it a coincidence that the Buddha reached enlightenment during meditation? A breakthrough experience in that light is a spiritual awakening. Living in that light is enlightenment.

Light is the most powerful energy in the universe and the most powerful energy within you. Light is also the only thing in the universe that illuminates. Simply put, light allows you to see. Without light, there is only darkness. This is both a literal fact and a spiritual metaphor. But there is a big difference between light and dark. Light is a physical entity in the sense that it's made of photons, which are bundles of energy. Darkness, on the other hand, is not made of anything. It has no substance or energy. Darkness is merely the absence of light. For darkness to exist, you must block out the light.

Try cupping your hands over your eyes until you can't see any light. Even though the light is still there, you can't see it because you're blocking it. The moment you remove that block, the darkness disappears. This is the illusion of darkness, also known as spiritual blindness. This is also the nature of light, or enlightenment. Light illuminates the darkness so you can see clearly. The more light there is, the more clearly you see and the easier your life becomes. The more darkness there is, the less clearly you see and the harder your life becomes, literally and metaphorically.

This leads to an important question. If more light allows you to see clearly, what is it that you are not seeing clearly now? For most people, there are three fundamental things they do not see clearly. First, they don't understand who they are or what their true nature is. They believe that who they are is a name, a body, a brain, a personality, and a culmination of their experiences. This creates a false identity that is so prominent that they are oblivious to the true essence of their being. A belief in the soul is a poor substitute for knowing the soul.

Second, because they don't know their true nature, they miss the true nature of others. They continue to operate at the level of judgment and otherness, for it is impossible to know and love others in a way you've never experienced for yourself. Their love remains conditional because they know nothing else. Third, they miss the true nature and purpose of life. They live in an unconscious opposition to life, constantly bouncing between two versions of fear: clinging and resisting. As a result, their inner peace is dependent on circumstance, and they accept suffering as normal, all the while missing the path to transcend it.

Light is also *lite*, meaning it is not heavy. Since light is energy without mass, it does not weigh anything. This too is a literal fact and a spiritual metaphor. Jesus said, "Take my yoke upon you and learn of me, for I am meek and lowly in heart, and ye shall find rest unto your souls. For my yoke is easy, and my burden is light." Why is Jesus' burden light? What heaviness is he not carrying that you are? He transcended his ego, the primary source of all mental and emotional suffering. He didn't carry baggage from his past or worry about his future. He had no insecurity about who he was. He didn't harbor resentment towards anyone or anything. If you didn't carry any of that, how light would you be?

A yoke is a wooden crosspiece that is fastened around the necks of two animals so they can pull together. Jesus' invitation to take his yoke upon you is widely interpreted to mean that because his burden is light, he can carry more for you. However, spiritual teachers often speak in code, so when you're ready, you'll see the deeper meaning. Notice that Jesus is inviting you to take his yoke, not yours. Your yoke is too heavy. His yoke represents the spiritual path he wants to show you. He's not proposing to carry your weight because he can. He's saying that if you walk alongside him, he'll show you how to unburden yourself so you can find rest unto your soul now, in this lifetime. He'll teach you how to make your burden light because he knows how to offload it. He's going to save you from yourself. This is the nature of light and the nature of enlightenment. You carry less weight and your burdens become lite.

Light is also the fastest energy in the universe. It travels at a speed of 186,000 miles per second, which means it moves from one place to another virtually instantaneously. Many people who are enlightened can point to a specific experience that changed everything. They just know the truth instantly. How is that possible? Conventional thinking says that to know something, you must learn, study, and accumulate knowledge over time. Case in point, the Buddha was taught spiritual truths for years before his enlightenment. He also tried different spiritual practices. What was different about day 49 then?

The most obvious answer is that enlightenment was an experience that superseded everything he thought he knew, replacing it with the truth. He went in one way and came out another. This is gamma brainwaves skyrocketing. This is revelation. This is the download or instant knowing where there is no delay between information and experience. Enlightenment is what happens when you experience truth moving at the speed of light.

In the end, enlightenment will show you that light is all there is. There is nothing else. Light is what creates universes. Light is the power that governs them. Light is what created you, and that same light is everything that you are. You are a part of it, and it is inextricably part of you. What you know as reality is the physical manifestation of an eternal energy that never dies. You are one with that energy at all times whether you know it or not. Not knowing is spiritual darkness, a state of separation from all that is. However, separation is merely an illusion, for the moment you stop covering your eyes with your hands, the light will be there.

Are you beginning to understand what enlightenment is? If you said no, you are actually starting to get it. It's all still just a finger pointing to the moon. What you need now is a roadmap. No, better yet, you need a flight plan. To become enlightened, you must go to the moon for yourself. The rest of this book will be that flight plan. Before you go further though, you should know what sacrifices are required to reach enlightenment. You may think that you must sell your possessions, forsake the world, and become a monk. Although that could accelerate your spiritual growth, external changes are really meant to produce an internal transformation. How about you skip straight to the internal transformation?

In reference to enlightenment, Jesus said, "it's easier for a camel to pass through the eye of the needle than it is for a rich man to enter the kingdom of God." On the surface, this sounds like an indictment against wealth. A deeper spiritual meaning is that it's hard for a rich man to let go of his identity as a rich man. Deeper still is the metaphor that to enter the kingdom of God, to reach enlightenment, you must mentally and emotionally let go of anything and everything you've accumulated in this life, for a cup that is full cannot be filled.

Letting go requires something more subtle and delicate than discipline or willpower. It requires surrender. To become enlightened, you must surrender who you think you are. You must surrender what you think you know. You must surrender your need for control, your pride, and your ego. That's the price of admission. In exchange, you enter a state within light. You become enlightened. That is where you'll find peace that surpasses all understanding and experience heaven on earth.

CHAPTER TWO

LOSE YOURSELF TO FIND YOURSELF

"The 'you' who you think you are does not exist."

- Alan Watts

Motivational speakers and self-help books often point out that the only thing stopping you from getting what you want is you. The basic idea is that if you change certain aspects of yourself, like your mentality, motivation level, or skill set, the world is yours for the taking. This is a great strategy for attaining just about anything in life except enlightenment. It is true that the only thing stopping you from becoming enlightened is you, however, the problem is that there's nothing you can change about yourself that will help. No matter who you become, you will still be the problem. To become enlightened, you do not change yourself. You get rid of yourself. Physical death is not required, but you must go through a spiritual death of sorts. The main issue is that you think you know who you are, but you don't.

What you know as *you* is merely a compilation of thoughts, a mental construct, an idea of who you are. You're so familiar and attached to this you that you don't even realize it's not you. That's who has to go. After you've died, your spiritual tombstone will read, "here lies the person you thought you were."

"Lose yourself to find yourself" is the best description of how you die spiritually. You must let go of who you think you are to uncover who you truly are. In scripture, this is giving up your natural man to be reborn of the spirit. If you successfully lose everything that is not you, what is leftover must be the real you. Think of it as a deconstruction process that removes layers of protections that stifle your authenticity, or an unmasking process that reveals your face for the first time. You've worn this mask and these protective layers for so long that you've forgotten you were even wearing them. If you want to know what is underneath, you must take them off.

This chapter is dedicated to helping you identify and shed each layer, one at a time. You'll also become aware of the mask, which is the first step towards removing it. Chapter three will show you exactly how the mask formed and how it works, so you don't fall into the trap of putting it back on. Subsequent chapters will show you how to remove it entirely. The path to enlightenment goes straight through you, but not the you that you think you are. That you must die. Do not worry. It will be your choice. It's always your choice. Don't volunteer to die for the sake of dying. Die so you can be reborn, to be your true Self.

Imagine that you've been asked to speak to a small audience for fifteen minutes. All they want to know is who you are. You've got weeks to prepare so you think about what would give them a comprehensive understanding of what makes you, *you*. You should probably start with your name, which is your most basic identifier. Perhaps you tell them how old you are, your relationship status, or whether you have kids or not. Do you tell them what you do for work or share some of your passions and hobbies?

What about your childhood? Maybe tell them about where you grew up. Share some early memories that mean something to you. Of course, you should tell them about the special people who have influenced you the most. What about your character and values? Those are foundational to who you are. Do you share some painful memories from your past that hurt you, even changed you? Maybe share some success stories or lessons you've learned. Although it might be controversial, you could share your religious beliefs or political leanings. You can't forget your personality either. Suppose you tell them that you are kind, but sometimes you lose your temper. Or that you're friendly, but you also like to be alone.

As you prepare, you realize that fifteen minutes isn't enough time. How do you sum up all that's happened to you, all that you've done, all your thoughts, feelings, dreams, beliefs, relationships, memories…really the entire experience of being you, in fifteen minutes? Nevertheless, this is how most people would prepare for a speech about who they are.

An enlightened person would do something quite different. First, they would not prepare because they don't need to. Second, they would stand in silence for fifteen minutes while the audience misses the point entirely. If the audience begged them, "please, tell us who you are, just one sentence." The enlightened person would say two words and the audience would still miss the point entirely. This is a person who knows exactly who they are. Once you understand the significance of this, you will reach enlightenment too.

In the spirit of losing yourself to find yourself, it's time to begin deconstructing your identity so you can uncover your true Self. Start with an easy identity to let go of, like your name. Does your name have anything to do with who you are? Someone gave you a name when you were born, but they could have named you anything. You know yourself as John or Mary, but you could just as easily have been Mark or Julie. In fact, you can decide right now to go by whatever name you choose. All you must do is tell people what you want to be called and just like that, you've got a new name.

To make it official, legally change your name with the government. Then your driver's license and passport will confirm that you are now someone else. Inside, wouldn't you be exactly the same? You can confidently say that your name is not who you are because you exist no matter what name you were given, or if you didn't have one at all. Keep going by whatever name suits you. Just don't think it has anything to do with who you are.

Does your age have anything to do with who you are? Imagine that you were stranded on a deserted island for the rest of your life with no way to keep track of time. It wouldn't take long for one day to blend into the next, let alone the months and years. You'd practically stop thinking about time altogether. The longer that went on, the less bearing you would have on how much time had passed. Suppose you were stranded on that island as a child, before you had a strong grasp of the concept of time. If fifty years passed, you wouldn't have a clue how old you were. If you guessed, you could be off by years, even decades. Yet, you would still exist.

The reason a five-year-old knows they are five is because they are told they are five. It's no different for a seventy-five-year-old. Age, at least in terms of time, is just a number in the mind. It's an interesting reference point, but it has nothing to do with the fundamental nature of your existence. The one who experiences what it's like to be five is the same one who will experience what it's like to be seventy-five. Age is a number, not a core component of your self-identity.

When you look in the mirror each morning, who do you see? You, right? For most of human history, the only way you could see yourself was through reflections in water or from a polished metal. It wasn't until the 15th century that mirrors became widely available and human beings could see themselves accurately. Imagine what it would be like to see yourself for the first time. You might laugh, cry, or stare with childlike curiosity.

You'd think, "so this is what I look like." Prior to that moment, you would never have associated your appearance with who you are.

Contrast that to today. You see yourself in a mirror more times in one day than many of your ancestors saw themselves during their lifetime. This frequent exposure to your appearance gives you the impression that what you look like has something to do with who you are. What if you were in a terrible accident that disfigured your face? You would look in the mirror the next morning and think, "this is not me."

In reality, your face would be different, but you would not be different. Although this is a dramatic example, it's not dissimilar from what happens as you age; the timeline is just longer. A photograph of you at age eight will look nothing like a photograph of you when you are eighty. These two versions of you are hardly comparable. However, because you look in the mirror so often, and because you age slowly, you don't notice your appearance changing. That's why your reflection always looks like you even though you change drastically over time. As convincing as the mirror is, don't fall for it. Your size, shape, and skin color are just a facade. Appearance is a shallow substitute for true identity.

When people ask what you do for work, you may say something like, "I'm a real estate agent," or "I'm a teacher." If you work a full-time job for most of your adult years, you'll spend a large portion of your life at work. It can seem like your job becomes synonymous with who you are. In some cases, people may even call you by your job title instead of using your name, Doctor or Coach being examples. But you only have to get fired, switch careers, or retire to see that your job is merely what you do for work. Whether you have your dream job, a job you hate, or no job at all, it has nothing to do with your core identity.

Similarly, money and possessions don't have anything to do with who you are. Driving a luxury car, living in a mansion, or wearing expensive clothes can make you feel like you're special. This is the illusion that wealth can somehow enhance who you are. Conversely, it is the false belief that being poor makes you less than you are. You can go from rags to riches or lose everything in a financial crisis or natural disaster, but you will still be you. Death will take it all anyway, so let go of any mental and emotional attachments now.

As much as you love your family and friends, it's easy to see why they are literally not you. Practically speaking, a family is a group of individuals that are related to one another. The key word being individuals. You may look like each other, share countless memories, and even have similar DNA, but you are your own person. Being single or married does not define you, nor does being a parent. You can have a best friend and an impressive social life, but it doesn't have anything to do with who you are. Self-identity is about yourself and no one else.

Are you seeing the pattern? If any component of your life can be removed, and you are still you, then that component was never you in the first place. If you ever wonder whether something is innate to who you are, ask yourself, "would I exist without this?" Would you exist without your education, religion, or beliefs? Would you exist without your addiction or patriotism? Would you exist without your successes or failures? If you think any of these components are integral to who you are, you have unconsciously linked your self-identity to things that are not actually you. This is what it means to lose yourself to find yourself.

If there is one thing that makes you who you are, surely it would be your unique personality. The dictionary defines your personality as the traits or qualities that give you a distinct character. As much as you may think that your personality is woven into the very fabric of your being, it isn't. In 2015, a study was published with the title "Sixteen Going on Sixty-six." The researchers wanted to know if people's personalities change over time. They followed almost two thousand participants for fifty years, regularly administering personality tests and tracking changes in universal traits—attributes like confidence, maturity, sensitivity, and desire for social interaction.

Researchers discovered that people's personalities don't change much over short periods of time, say three years. However, their personalities changed quite a bit over longer periods of time. A decade, for example. Participants in the study showed reliable change to one or more of their personality traits over the fifty-year period.

Have you ever known someone who had a traumatic experience years ago and they've never been the same? A young soldier full of energy and passion may come back from war with anxiety and fear. They don't seem like the same person. As a matter of fact, they are the same person. They're just behaving and expressing themselves differently. If they go to therapy and heal, their original personality may re-emerge, but it is the same person who existed before the war, after the war, during healing, and after healing. Similarly, think about a painfully shy person who overcomes their fear and becomes outgoing. The same person exhibits both traits, meaning neither trait was a core element of their identity.

If you can lose one trait and adopt another, clearly neither trait is you. Your personality is fluid, malleable, and ever-changing. No matter what traits you exhibit, there is a continuity of Self that underlies any expression of personality. As the anonymous, snarky quote goes, "you are unique in your own way, just like everyone else." In other words, personality is not your true identity.

For many people, the hardest identity to let go of is their attachment to their past. As you look back on your life, you may point to events or experiences that molded you into who you are. For example, maybe you haven't been quite the same since you got your heart broken all those years ago. When your parents got divorced, did you stop feeling and shut down? Remember how proud you were when you crossed the finish line of that 10k? All of these memories give you a sense of who you are, which would suggest that your past is forever linked to your identity.

Have you ever wondered why you remember certain things and not others? After all, you've experienced millions of events during your lifetime, yet you only remember a very small percentage of what has happened. You remember your first kiss, but you may struggle to remember anything that happened last Tuesday.

Why do some events stand out when others fade almost as quickly as they happen? If you analyze your memories, you'll discover that most memories are linked with strong emotions. Painful, traumatic memories stand out, as do blissful, happy moments.

Memories are not just digital files with no meaning. They are married to powerful senses and emotions. In a literal sense, the past leaves mental, emotional, and physical impressions. If those impressions are strong enough, even a single event or experience can get stuck, thus altering your sense of Self or becoming a defining moment in your life. For better or worse, the idea is that the past changed you, therefore it defines you.

Think of a high school football star who doesn't know who he is without going back to the good old days. His identity is stuck in the past. Think of a person who can't forgive themselves for something they've done. Their so-called sins define who they are, however long ago the mistakes were made. Because of what they did, they believe they are a bad person. Therefore, they are defined by their past, which means their self-identity is their past.

Healing is the process of dissolving the mental, emotional, and physical residue from the past. The events and experiences themselves do not change, but the meaning and feelings surrounding them does. In this way, you let go of the past and realize it is no longer part of your identity, which means it never was. You cannot be an experience. You cannot be an event. You are the one who experiences. You were you before these memorable events. You will still be you no matter what experiences you have in the future. The only way the past can define you is if you look to the past to tell you who you are.

Having a body is one of the most primal parts of being human. You experience the world through your senses, specifically taste, touch, smell, sight and sound. The ability to move your body also gives you a sense of control, suggesting that your body is either critical to who you are, or at least an extension of who you are. With that said, suppose you were completely paralyzed, losing all feeling and mobility. Then imagine that you also went blind and deaf, and lost your sense of taste and smell.

Obviously, your quality of life would be non-existent, but if someone took care of you in this state, you could survive. Sadly, Lou Gehrig's disease isn't far off from this scenario. Even so, this example is really meant to tee up a very important question. If your body no longer works but your mind is fully functional, are you still "inside?"

The answer is yes. You, the person, the consciousness, would still be inside your useless body. Think of it like being inside a car. You don't think that you are the car. You know you are inside. Similarly, do not think that you are your body. You are inside. To illustrate this further, if you believe in an afterlife, you must also believe there is a part of you that will live long after your body turns to dust. This eternal version of you exists with or without your body. Why? Because you are not your body.

The list of things that are not you is getting longer. You are not your name, age, appearance, job, family, friends, nationality, education, religion, beliefs, personality, past, or your body. What could possibly be left? Fortunately, you only have to shed one more identity. It is the most important identity you must let go of if you want to become enlightened. If you can grasp the truth and significance of the next several paragraphs, you will be at the starting point of the most spiritual journey a human being can take. It's time to unmask.

If your body no longer works but you are still inside, there is only one logical conclusion you can come to. Your consciousness, this inner you, must exist in your mind. Another way of saying it is that you are your mind. Scientists estimate that you have somewhere between 60,000 and 80,000 thoughts per day. Some thoughts are meaningful, true, and useful. Others are random, incorrect, and pointless. Some thoughts make you feel good. Others make you suffer. A good question to ask is, why does your mind think the thoughts it does? A more profound question is, which of the thoughts that you think are you?

Suppose you're driving and you see a homeless man at the stop sign. You think to yourself, "I should start volunteering at the homeless shelter." It's a wonderful, noble thought. As you keep driving, you see someone you can't stand and think, "I could run them over." Of course, you know that you're not actually going to run them over, but you did think it. Which one of those thoughts is you? Are you the volunteer or the murderer? If you consider yourself to be a kind person, you may lean towards the noble thought. It aligns more with who you believe you are. You're not the type of person who would run someone over, so that was just a random thought you can discard. It didn't mean anything. This is a metaphor for how many people view their thoughts. They think, "this thought is me" and "that thought is not me."

With some low-level scrutiny, it's easy to see that this is not a logical way to view your thoughts. You can't just accept certain thoughts as true while ignoring all the others as if they don't exist. Where do all those thoughts you dismiss come from anyway? How do you decide which thoughts are coming from you and which ones aren't? There are some obvious holes in viewing your thoughts this way.

The next plausible answer is that you must be all of your thoughts. Every thought is coming from you, even though you don't want to admit it. The irrational, crazy, dark thoughts must be you too. You are the volunteer and the murderer. Here's your dilemma. Do you believe that some of your thoughts are you but others are not? Or do you believe that you are all of your thoughts?

To know the answer for yourself, try a simple exercise. After this paragraph, close your eyes for thirty seconds and observe your thoughts by listening to the voice in your head. Just make a mental note of what thoughts pop up, however random they seem. You may think of something you need to do or worry whether you're a murderer. It doesn't matter. Just observe. If you think at any point, "I'm not having any thoughts," that's also a thought. Try it now. Close your eyes and observe your thoughts for about thirty seconds. When you're done, open your eyes and continue reading.

During the exercise, you observed your thoughts as they came across your mind. Ask yourself, "who is the one who observed the thoughts?" In order for you to observe something, two things must be present. An observer who has something to observe. For example, you are reading this book, which makes you the observer. This book is the object you are observing. If you look at a building, you are the observer. The building is the object you are observing. How do you know that you are not this book or the building that you see? Because you are the one observing them, obviously. This is exactly what you did in the exercise. You observed your thoughts. You are the observer. Thoughts were the objects that you observed. On the surface, this may seem like nothing more than an interesting party trick, but you cannot underestimate the magnitude of what you just learned.

To get an idea, go back to the original example. You're driving and you see the homeless man at the stop sign. You think, "I should start volunteering at the homeless shelter." You drive a little further and see someone you just can't stand and think, "I could run them over." Which of the two thoughts are you? One of them or both of them? The answer is neither. You are the one who observes both thoughts. Out of the 60,000-80,000 thoughts you have each day, not one is you. You are not some of the thoughts. You are not all of them. You are none of them.

Nothing that the voice in your head has ever said was you. Nothing it will say will ever be you. Nothing it is saying right now is you. If this is a revelation to you, it means that your whole life you have mistaken the voice in your head as who you are. You thought it was you talking in there, you thinking in there, when the whole time you were actually the one listening and observing. Your entire self-identity is built on the premise that the voice in your head is you, when it is not you.

Are you thinking right now, "this can't be true." If so, who is the one saying that? Who is the one listening? To know the truth, all you must do is close your eyes, observe your thoughts, and ask, who is aware of these thoughts? You are. If you think your name is Mary, that is a thought, which means that thought isn't you. If you think you are a good person or a bad person, those are thoughts too. Where does the past exist? As a memory, which is a stored thought. Where does your personality exist? As a thought, a mental concept. This you, that isn't really you, exists as a thought. It's only an idea of yourself. You are merely thinking about you, which means you are not getting your information from the one who really knows.

The real you exists independently of all thoughts because the real you is aware of all thoughts. You are not the voice in your head. You never have been. You never will be. To understand and experience the separation between you and your thoughts is what it means to become spiritually awakened.

To make this concept more palpable, imagine giving a surgeon the task of dissecting your brain in an attempt to find *you* inside. They would find your frontal lobe, amygdala, cerebellum, hypothalamus, etc., but they would not find the source of consciousness or awareness. A brain scan can't detect or monitor it either. This does not mean that consciousness isn't real, or that you do not exist. It's that you do not exist in the way you think you do, as a human.

Think of consciousness like a digital file on a computer. You can dismantle the computer with a set of screwdrivers, scouring the hardware for the file, but you won't find it. The file is invisible in a sense, yet it is real, just like consciousness. Technology may one day advance enough to reveal the invisible nature of consciousness; however, this elusive inner you is the centerpiece of spirituality.

Even though science cannot detect consciousness right now, you can. Why? Because you are it. The odds are that you've just never explored this part of you. Only by metaphorically stripping away all your external layers, your temporary human components, will you come to know the purest form of who you are. Your false Self must die so your true Self can be reborn.

Who were you before the conditioning, expectations, knowledge, beliefs, and rigid self-identity got in the way? What about you would be exactly the same if you were born into a different time, a different body, a different family, a different culture, and you had a completely different life? Who are you without the titles and labels other people have given you, or the ones you've given yourself?

If you feel like you're having an identity crisis after reading this chapter, you're learning that surrender isn't as easy as waving a white flag. Surrender is often a disorienting, scary process of shedding layers of yourself. "Lose yourself to find yourself" sounds catchy as a platitude, but in practice it can feel like a loss, a crisis, even death. This is one reason why few people reach enlightenment. They are unwilling to sit with discomfort and uncertainty as they surrender to the unknown.

If you can make peace with being lost for a short time, you'll create enough space for your true Self to emerge. Whatever fear and insecurity you may feel along the journey will eventually be replaced with a bulletproof confidence that is beyond any identity your mind can comprehend. Beneath the clothes and the mask, you are the real deal, the genuine article, a bonafide eternal being who looked in the mirror and mistakenly thought you were human.

CHAPTER THREE

THE FOUNDATION BUILT ON SAND

"And every one that heareth these sayings of mine, and doeth them not, shall be likened unto a foolish man, which built his house upon the sand: and the rain descended, and the floods came, and the winds blew, and beat upon that house; and it fell: and great was the fall of it."

-Jesus

A humbling step on your path to enlightenment is the realization that you are the foolish man who built his house upon the sand. You built your house, your self-identity, on a foundation that is not solid. Don't worry, that's what everyone around you did too. Most of humanity still does. Regardless, it's now time to ask some important questions. If everything you thought you were is not actually you, then what is that convincing pseudo-identity? What is this house built on the sand that appears so solid? The self-identity you've built upon the sand is your ego. Ego is one of the least understood parts of the human experience, yet there is nothing that will negatively impact the quality of your life more than your ego. Trying to describe the ego is like trying to describe air. You can't see air. You can't grab it, nor can you really explain its ineffable qualities.

However, when you understand atoms, molecules, and compounds, something invisible turns out to be as real as any physical object you can see or touch. Likewise, this invisible entity called the ego can't be found or extracted, yet it's tactics and impact will be familiar to you because it has been your lived experience. In the same way that you breathe whether you know the air is there or not, you engage with your ego whether you know it or not.

To understand ego, start with a basic definition: Ego is mistaking the voice in your head as who you are. In other words, ego = voice in your head. Voice in your head = ego. Throughout this chapter, the terms ego and voice in your head will be used interchangeably to solidify this connection in your mind. This voice is the single greatest cause of your personal suffering, as well as the collective suffering of humanity. Ego is where all your fears, anxieties, insecurities, judgments, reactions, limiting beliefs, wounds, traumas, and fragile self-identity come from. Think of your ego as a separate entity living in your head, because it is an entity of sorts—or at least it thinks it is. That's why ego, like enlightenment, is a paradox. Ego is incredibly real until it is not real at all. That's why it is also referred to as the illusory Self. Another way of saying this is that ego is the illusion of Self.

As long as you think that the voice in your head is you, your ego is incredibly real. This voice influences and controls your thoughts, feelings, and behavior without you ever suspecting that something is amiss. The moment you stop identifying with the voice in your head, ego vanishes into the illusion that it is. Becoming enlightened is directly tied to your ability to transcend your ego and Self-realize. More on that in later chapters.

The structural mechanics of the ego are quite straightforward. You have a brain, which is the physical, tangible organ in your skull. Ego is an invisible extension of the brain, a vocalizing mechanism of the brain. Think of it as the brain's voice. This voice is not you any more than your big toe is you. How do you know? You can observe the voice just like you can observe your big toe, provided you maintain objectivity. The problem is that sometimes you get so lost in your mind that you lose objectivity, to the point where you don't realize you're lost. Your suffering in this life is directly proportional to how lost you get in your mind, in ego.

Your ego formed at a very young age, and it did so for a very good reason. The primary function of your brain is survival. Not peace, joy, or happiness, but survival. Your brain constantly scans for threats so it can avoid physical pain and, ultimately, death. Fear is the emotion the brain uses to get your attention so you can defend and protect yourself. As a child, your brain discovered two other forms of pain, namely mental and emotional pain, or what you could call pain of the psyche. This pain stems from judgment, rejection, abandonment, neglect, and not feeling safe.

Mental and emotional pain doesn't have to come from extreme trauma; it's much more delicate. A helpless infant feels abandoned when a parent doesn't comfort them when they cry. A child receives love when they behave like their parents want them to, only to have that love withheld when the child doesn't comply. Hurtful words, being picked last, or enduring bullying cause pain too. Obviously, blatant abuse and neglect are incredibly harmful, often inflicting lasting damage on the psyche. Mental and emotional pain is the birthplace of this inner protector known as ego.

No matter your upbringing, everyone receives two detrimental messages from family or society in subtle and not so subtle ways. First, you are not good enough as you are. Second, love is not safe because it is conditional. This is the root of the universal human fear, the fear of not being good enough. Your ego says that if you are not good enough, you are not worthy of love.

Since your ego's primary function is to protect against mental and emotional pain, you may assume that the voice in your head is protecting you. You should remember, however, that the ego is its own entity. It is not you. As an extension of the brain, it also prioritizes survival above everything else. Whose survival? Its own survival. In the same way that the brain is afraid of pain and death, your ego is afraid of pain and its own death. So much so that it will make you think that if your ego dies, you will die.

Picture a tiny balloon floating in your head with an image of your face on it. This balloon is filled with all your thoughts about who you are. This is your self-concept or image of yourself. Letting the air out of that balloon slowly is ego dissolution. Popping that balloon in one shot is ego death. The closer you get to ego death, the more mental and emotional buttons your ego will push to terrify you. Fear of death comes exclusively from your ego, which is why one of the hallmarks of enlightenment is a loss of the fear of death. The fact that your ego can dissolve or die means that you can live without your ego. The balloon dies, but you do not. More accurately, the balloon disappears because it only existed as an idea in the first place. There is no balloon.

Since the ego is afraid of mental and emotional pain, it creates an inner world it can control to insulate it from an outer world it cannot control. That's why the voice in your head talks so much. Thinking, judging, predicting, assuming, and analyzing helps the ego manage its fears by giving it a sense of control. Essentially, the ego creates a protective lens through which it sees the world. More personally, ego is the lens through which you see the world.

To illustrate this, imagine that you go parasailing with a friend on a beautiful summer day. You're five hundred feet above the ocean in a two-person harness, floating beneath a giant parachute that's being pulled by a small boat below. Your friend is looking at the turquoise water and white sandy beach, feeling like a bird flying through the cloudless sky. Meanwhile, you're thinking, "I hope the knot to the parachute doesn't come loose. If

I fell from this height, would I die? If I don't die, I wonder if there are sharks in the water." You're shaking in fear, desperate to get back on solid ground.

Notice that you and your friend are in the exact same objective reality. You're parasailing. Yet the reality you experience is completely different based on the filter of the mind. Practically speaking, parasailing is not thrilling or scary. Your ego's interpretation of reality makes it so.

In essence, your ego filters objective reality to create your personal reality. It's not merely distorting reality. It's literally creating its own version. This mind-made version is what you experience without realizing it. Parasailing is merely a metaphor for how you experience your entire life.

The implications are staggering when you consider that every interaction, situation, and experience you've ever had, from the mundane and benign to the terrifying and traumatic, was viewed through the lens of the ego. In other words, your personal reality is only real because you believe it is real, because you believe the voice in your head. You believed the voice when it told you parasailing was scary, and therefore it was.

Anything and everything the voice tells you is real, but only because you believe it. It's your truth, but it's not *the* truth. It's your reality, but it's not true reality. If you do not believe or react to the voice in your head, it is a meaningless illusion that has no power to make you suffer. This is the bedrock truth of enlightenment: you do not suffer your life—you suffer your mind.

All the while you thought that the source of suffering was "out there" when it was really "in here." If you misidentify the real cause of suffering, what chance do you have of ending it? In the most stealthy, manipulative way, the ego essentially blames reality for your suffering, successfully diverting attention away from the real culprit, itself. Reality will never conform to the ego's desires, which means the end of suffering can only come by addressing the true source of suffering: ego.

The fallacy of the ego is that if it can think everything through, choose all the right things, and always be prepared for what's coming, it can avoid pain. In some cases, that's true. But because most people think their suffering is caused by life situations and experiences, they try to curate and control their external world so everything will one day be in its proper place. Then they will be happy, find peace, and enjoy life. Of course, this utopia never comes. The paradox is that by trying to avoid mental and emotional pain, the ego lives in protection and fear, which is mental and emotional pain. As long as you experience life through the protective lens of your ego, you will never end your suffering. You will never be free.

Your ego always protects itself under the guise of protecting you. Like a husband who supposedly protects his wife only to make her dependent on him, your ego uses fear to control you while simultaneously telling you it's keeping you safe. The best word to describe the ego is insidious, which means to move in a subtle, cunning way, but with grave effect towards one's destruction. Insidious comes from the Latin word insidiae, which translates as ambush. While it would be accurate to say the ego is a protector, the voice in your head is not looking out for you.

Fear is the self-defense mechanism the ego uses to protect its existence, never hesitating to use scare tactics in devious, deceitful ways. In reality, an illusory Self is peddling illusory fear, meaning that fear is an illusion, no different from the ego itself. Be that as it may, most of humanity unconsciously gives up control to the ego because it is clearly good at hiding its existence, let alone its tactics. The voice is very convincing, otherwise no one would listen. Ego embodies a popular acronym for F.E.A.R., which is False Evidence Appearing Real.

Fear-based thoughts are where your ego starts, but thoughts on their own are usually not enough to change behavior. However, when thoughts are linked to feelings, fear becomes very real. The brain and the body are telling you, sometimes screaming at you, that you're in danger. Physiologically, the body doesn't know the difference between real fear and ego-generated fear, so it reacts the same way. Your ego uses this to its advantage by exploiting the body's fight-or-flight systems.

Think of a person who suffers from panic attacks in social situations. There is no physical danger, which means their fear is purely psychological. The ego pulls the right mental and emotional strings to force the body into protection mode. Even mental health struggles like anxiety and depression are physical responses to the ego's fears. Whereas anxiety is protection in the form of bracing for what could happen, always ready to defend or fight, depression is protection in the form of shutting down, a way to run away and hide. Both strategies are the ego's way of trying to protect against real or perceived pain, which creates or prolongs the pain.

The ego fabricates a problem and searches for a solution with no real intention of ending the suffering. In fact, this futile chase is the suffering. If that manipulation continues for weeks, months, or years, the ego successfully trains the body to be hypersensitive or numb to feeling altogether. Either way, the ego and the body live in a constant, miserable state of protection.

Many people are tortured by their own mind and body, largely unaware that the ego is manipulating reality in the background. The suffering is real, but only because they believe it is real. They've followed the ego so far down the rabbit hole that they got lost, to the point where the illusion is indistinguishable from reality. It becomes their reality. Waking up to the illusion is ego death. Unless you are in physical danger, fear and its derivatives are always an illusion, however real it feels. Insecurity, neediness, guilt, shame, jealousy, envy, defensiveness, self-centeredness, second guessing, and overconfidence are all protections against the core fear of the ego, the fear of not being enough.

Narcissism is a perfect example of the ego going to extreme lengths to protect itself. That's why narcissists are known for having big egos. Narcissists are usually smart, entitled, self-centered, brash, powerful, and devastatingly insecure. That's why they compensate. Deep down, they are deathly afraid of not being enough; their bravado is masking their greatest fear. Facing the possibility of not being enough is too painful a prospect to even consider, hence the inability to self-reflect or admit fault. Remember, ego death feels like real death.

Although narcissists are judged harshly, those who find self-worth and positive self-image through external variables employ the same egoic tactics, just with less collateral damage. Many people use success, money, intelligence, talents, accomplishments, beauty, and other social currencies to prove their worth. Their unconscious belief is that something outside will make them whole inside. This is a donkey chasing a carrot that is always just out of reach. It's the ego trying to outrun the fear of not being enough by proving it's not true. If I am ___, then I am enough.

Another extreme form of ego that doesn't get the bad rep of narcissism is self-hatred. Those who self-loath are the other side of the same coin. The only difference between someone who hates themselves and a narcissist is one admits to feeling inadequate while the other is in denial. Both live with the same fear, and as a result, they have big egos that are running and ruining their lives.

The ego will take on a negative self-image just as easily as a positive one and defend it with equal passion. Try giving a genuine compliment to someone with low self-esteem. They will either downplay or dismiss it because it doesn't match their image of who they are. Whereas half the population tries to outrun the fear of not being enough, the other half owns it, taking it on as their self-identity. This is why many people have low self-worth and a poor self-image. If they can wallow in self-pity, they always have an excuse to play small, never having to risk rejection, failure, or disappointment, which would only confirm what they already believe: they are not enough.

As much as their conscious mind says it wants the pain to stop, the ego needs to keep the pain as a protection. To let go of a negative self-image is also ego death, no less terrifying to face than a narcissist confronting their fear of not being enough. A person who thinks that they are not good enough can't bear the thought of finally feeling good enough, only for it to be taken away. Living in hell is less painful than touching heaven and having to come back.

Victim mentality is a powerful egoic identity based around what happened to you, or what was done to you. The ego clings to a past trauma, injustice, or tragedy, forming an almost impenetrable defense against future pain. Reliving the pain is a way to ensure it doesn't happen again, yet the person continues to suffer even though the experience is over. Therefore, the ego is in full control.

Those with victim mentality often look for continuous validation for their pain under the guise of healing, which is a crafty way the ego reinforces its identity as a victim. Pain = protection, which means giving up victim mentality would expose them to the possibility of getting hurt again. Victim mentality, narcissism, depression, anxiety, addiction, and even some physical illnesses are elaborate protections to insulate and cocoon the ego. Ego will hide behind anything that will protect it while burying its larger fears in the subconscious. The bigger the wound, the bigger the protection. The bigger the protection, the bigger the ego.

Of course, most people are not narcissists, self-loathers, or victims. There is a spectrum of high functioning people who have successful lives and relationships, largely unaware or uninhibited by their ego. Perhaps you fit in this camp. It would be natural to question whether you should care about your ego if it's not making you suffer in obvious ways. High-functioning people are at high risk of completely identifying with their ego without realizing it, as they often find their self-identity in stability, accomplishments, social status, or belief systems. In other words, ability, likability, success, and certainty is their identity. They think they've made it in some sense, unconsciously believing that they have successfully outrun the fear of not being enough.

Their sense of Self can continue so long as they perform, but it's a house of cards. Oftentimes, a major life event like divorce, bankruptcy, death of a close family member, unemployment, or diagnosis forces them to question everything they thought they knew about themselves or the world. The house eventually falls, revealing a fragile, egoic identity built on the world affirming their worth and sense of Self.

Ego death is painful for this group because they do not know who they are without external variables propping them up. Experiences that rock someone to the core can be catalysts for transcending the ego if they resist the urge to reconstruct their self-image and avoid doubling down on their desire to control reality. The spiritual reason why everyone should care about understanding ego is because ego represents the barrier between themselves and true spirituality. For most people, spirituality is largely about what they believe. A belief, however, is nothing more than a thought that you think is true. It exists in the mind.

In contrast, spirituality is defined as the quality of being concerned with the human spirit. Remember, ego is misidentifying who you are as the voice in your head. If you are oblivious to your ego, you are identified exclusively with your ego, which means you must also be oblivious to your spirit, regardless of how much you believe in it. High functioning or not, true spirituality can only be found on the other side of ego.

Another way the ego transforms fear into protection is through self-sabotage. The voice in your head is a master saboteur, carefully creating diversions and smoke screens designed to keep you safe, while robbing you of your biggest dreams and desires. The things you want the most represent the greatest risk, so the voice in your head often creates a lesser fear to obscure a deeper one. By chasing a ghost, your ego avoids the true demon it's afraid of. In this way, self-sabotage serves its purpose.

Nowhere is this more prevalent than in intimate relationships. All human beings crave to be fully seen and loved just as they are. But to risk being fully seen is to risk the ultimate rejection, a confirmation of your ego's greatest fear of not being enough. The person you love the most can also hurt you the most, which makes true love one of the most triggering things there is. Vulnerability is often too scary for your ego so it will hedge against the risk by creating stories and narratives that feel incredibly real. These stories are nothing more than elaborate distractions to protect the ego.

The voice in your head could ruminate on thoughts about your old high school lover to make you question whether you married the right person. Your ego may create baseless jealousies that put you into fear and your partner on the defense, successfully putting distance in your relationship. Even though you don't like how you look, you keep eating too much because, subconsciously, your insecurity about your weight is protecting you from enjoying intimacy.

Have you convinced yourself that you don't feel what other people feel because you're different, when you're just afraid to be vulnerable? Secrets weigh you down with guilt and shame, yet those feelings ensure that you never let anyone in. Like a con man who smiles while picking your pocket, your ego supposedly protects you while sabotaging true love. Protection to the ego is self-sabotage to the soul.

Self-sabotage extends to every other aspect of your life too. Playing small insulates you from criticism but suffocates your dreams. Being a chameleon means you never make waves, but blending in conceals your authenticity. Procrastinating doing things that would change your life is easier, but it means your life will never change. Author Brianna West writes, "Self-sabotage is simply the presence of an unconscious need that is being fulfilled by the self-sabotaging behavior."

Every unconscious need is rooted in your ego's insatiable need for reassurance that it is good enough, all the while self-sabotaging any attempts to fill the void. Your ego is stuck in a never-ending catch-22, unable to self-realize because it is only an illusion of the mind, yet it is dependent on siphoning your life energy to keep the illusion going. Problems provide it with the fuel and purpose it needs to survive.

Your ego doesn't have control over the external world, so it goes inward to chew and churn on problems internally. Worrying about what did happen or what could happen helps your ego prepare for the worst. Needing to be in control is often mistaken as a personality trait when the ego is simply afraid. This is why many people live with some level of negativity, frustration, dissatisfaction, anxiety, or underlying sense of angst. The irony is that by living in fear, your ego suffers all the same. You suffer all the same.

Always on alert, the voice in your head rarely allows you to feel inner peace, if at all. One reason drugs and alcohol are so prevalent is because people feel relief from their problems. In reality, they feel relief from the voice in their head, which is the source of their problems. Even when your ego does solve a problem, it will feel temporary relief before moving the goalpost once again. It needs problems to exist, and in an imperfect world, there are limitless options to choose from.

Deliverance for your ego is always at a future time and destination that is just out of reach. In fact, your ego is completely dependent on time for its existence, which is why it holds tightly to the past and looks to the future. This, too, is born from its fear of a reality it cannot control. It cannot stand the present moment because it can't predict or control it. The past gives your ego an archive of what hurt it in the past. The future represents a day when all its fears will be alleviated. However, your ego always carries fear from the past into the present. Therefore, the future is sadly predictable.

The present is reduced to a mental and emotional limbo, an in-between state of thinking and feeling that "when this happens, then I'll be happy." As a result, the present moment is nothing more than a constant reminder of lack and discontent. Like a weary traveler, your ego never arrives at the peace and happiness it so desperately wants. Neither will you if you do not escape its power. This present moment is the only time where real life is happening.

In the mind, the past is made up of former present moments stacked one on top of the other. Although these moments exist as memories in the brain, they are no longer real because you cannot go back. The future is a projection that the brain assumes will exist, but it is not real either because you cannot jump ahead.

Your ego's dependence on creating an inner reality is thwarted by the present moment because your conscioussness, your soul, is what emerges when you are present. If only for a moment, you have severed the connection between you and your ego because you have actually engaged with true reality.

Now that you've learned what your ego is, where it formed, and how it operates, it's time to zoom out and revisit the basics. First, ego is the voice in your head. It is not you. It's just your brain talking. Second, when you misidentify who you are as that voice, when you believe it's narratives and stories, you are under the influence and control of your ego. This mind-made filter is the lens through which you see reality, which creates your reality. As a result, you do not suffer your life—you suffer your mind. Third, the ego runs on fear. It is afraid of death, pain, and the fear of not being enough. It uses thoughts to influence feelings, making everything seem real, thus deceiving you while using you as its energy source. Ego is nothing more than a convincing illusion.

What keeps the illusion going? The voice in your head needs you to listen to it, react to it, and give it any kind of attention. Continue believing all the narratives and stories it tells you. That validates its existence, making the illusion real, but only to you. As you try to get separation from your ego, it will sense you pulling away. It will talk more to make you feel like you will never escape its incessant thoughts. It will use every trigger and weapon in its arsenal to suck you back into "protection" through anxiety, fear, hurt, anger, insecurity, depression, dissatisfaction, or discontent. Why is it doing this?

To get you to identify with it in any way possible. If you keep reacting to the voice in your head as if it is a real entity, as if it's you, it has an endless supply of fuel, and the illusion lives on.

In this chapter, you've gotten a close-up of your ego and seen how the sausage is made. You can't unsee this, at least not if you want to become enlightened. Understanding your ego so you can go beyond it is a seismic spiritual shift. There's no going back. Knowing what you're up against can be overwhelming, especially when you consider the scale of your ego's deception and sabotage over your lifetime. This fragile, false Self is the foundation you built upon the sand. Your spiritual path includes watching it disintegrate.

Knowing this information may make you feel anger towards your ego. After all, it is the sole cause of your suffering. It stands directly in the way of your highest fulfillment and freedom. Over the coming weeks and months, you may become hyperaware of the voice in your head and how much it's making you suffer, only to feel helpless to stop it. Jesus described this stage when he said, "No man can serve two masters, for either he will hate the one and love the other, or else he will hold to the one, and despise the other." If you hate your ego, your ego has manipulated you once again. You will be angry at an illusory entity that needs you to identify with it in some way, in any way, to keep it alive.

Rather than anger, you should feel compassion for your ego. In a strange way, you understand its plight because it's been your plight. What you can't see now is that somewhere along your path to enlightenment, you'll feel gratitude for your ego because it was providing you with the exact amount of suffering you needed to wake up. This spiritual awakening will set you on a trajectory that ends in enlightenment. Once you're enlightened, you'll know that your life has played out exactly the way it was meant to. Remember that ego, like enlightenment, is a paradox. The very ego that appears to be hurting you is preparing you to transcend it.

CHAPTER FOUR

THE WAY FORWARD IS THROUGH

"The wound is the place where the light enters you."

-Rumi

In an ideal world, you would go straight from ego awareness to ego transcendence and end your suffering in one shot. However, that's like going from little league to the pros. Although it's possible to have a single experience that changes everything, it is rare. When it does happen, it often comes after a person has suffered so much that their mental model of reality breaks. These people transcend almost by accident because their only choices are death or total freedom. Continuing to suffer is no longer an option. It would be unwise to wish this for yourself or chase after a mystical experience that may never happen.

Think of the state of enlightenment as a river where there are neither rocks diverting the water, nor dams stopping the water from flowing freely. Water moves gently and peacefully without obstruction. Similarly, a person who is enlightened allows experiences, thoughts, and feelings to flow through them without obstructtion. Everything passes through. This is the state of no suffering. Unsurprisingly, this is the exact opposite of how most people live. Certain experiences, thoughts, and feelings get stuck. The more mental and emotional pain you suppress, the more rocks fill up in the river, restricting the natural flow.

Rocks represent your accumulated baggage, emotional wounds, limiting beliefs, traumas, and suppressed pain. You may have a few rocks that need to be removed or some giant boulders that are damming up the river. Regardless, a critical step between ego awareness and ego transcendence is healing. Healing is the process of removing the rocks. Transcendence is the ability to stop accumulating rocks for the rest of your life.

In a way, healing may sound like a counterintuitive step in your spiritual journey. The only part of you that has ever felt traumatized, hurt, rejected, abandoned, offended, or inadequate is your ego. Why heal the very entity that is responsible for all your pain? If you clench your fist as hard as you can for fifteen seconds, it isn't hard to release your hand back to a relaxed position.

However, if you clench your fist as hard as you can for two minutes, it will take much longer for your hand to release its grip. Likewise, the more pain you experience and suppress, the more your ego creates a fortress of protection that it will defend aggressively. Well before your ego can consider relinquishing its role as a protector, it must feel safe enough to put down its defenses. Healing helps the ego loosen its grip.

An enlightened person has a unique relationship with pain. They know that mental and emotional pain is incredibly spiritual, even sacred. Although they do not seek pain like a masochist, they honor its place in the human experience and its role in the eternal picture. Conversely, most of humanity tries to avoid pain at all costs. What about you? Do you label certain experiences, thoughts, or feelings as good and desirable while deeming others as bad and unwelcome? When painful things happen, do you brace, suppress, numb, deny, withdraw, or try to move on as quickly as possible? These strategies may appear to work in the short term, but this is how you accumulate rocks in the river.

Painful feelings do not disappear. They go dormant, leaving a trigger behind that must be avoided or worked around, just like water is forced to go around the rock.

Suppress your pain over many years and the river gets progressively littered with rocks, slowing the natural flow. Then you wake up at some point in your life and can't figure out why you're unhappy. You are afraid of what people think. You're afraid to be vulnerable, take a chance, lose control, fail, or give and receive love without holding back.

Ironically, you're afraid to be free because you could get hurt. In your desire to avoid pain, you've created a bigger problem. You're not just suffering from pain anymore. You're suffering from the fear of pain. Fear of suffering has become its own form of suffering—you're living in a mental prison of your own making. As long as fear is present in your life, you cannot be free.

Healing will free you from the pain of your past, but healing also serves as the training course that teaches you to stop being afraid of pain. That's the real problem. You're afraid of pain. The ego blames the event or experience from the past as the thing to be afraid of, but you're not really afraid of an event or experience. You're afraid of how it made you feel. In other words, you're afraid of a feeling. Your ego uses pain from your past to protect you from potential pain in the future, which causes pain in the present. When you are no longer afraid to feel pain, you're free. That is the end of suffering. Do you want to heal or transcend suffering once and for all? Why not do both?

Learning to feel and process pain is a sacred, spiritual skill known as transmutation. Transmutation means to change something into another form. In emotional terms, you start with pain and transmute it into peace. Start with trauma and transmute it into power. Whereas your two previous options were to suppress your pain or get overwhelmed by it, transmutation is to dive headfirst into your pain knowing that it can be refined, purified, and released to the point where there is no emotional residue. No more triggers. No more fear. No more pain. Go through the transmutation process a couple of times and you're hooked. Instead of running from pain, you welcome it because it becomes fuel for your ascension. Author Joseph Campbell inadvertently described transmutation perfectly when he said, "every feeling fully felt is bliss."

Some people are acutely aware that they need to heal. They have obvious wounds or patterns of behavior that are telltale signs of trauma. True victims can often point to specific events like rape, war, diagnosis, or the tragic death of a loved one. Physical, emotional, or sexual abuse can also warp the psyche and alter perceptions of reality. In order to cope, trauma victims may turn to addiction, self-harm, suicidality, promiscuity, violence, or other maladaptive coping strategies that compound their wounds. They suffer greatly because of their life experiences, but also because their egoic protections are so prevalent that they cannot enjoy life or relationships. Trauma victims are worthy of great compassion and empathy. Healing is their best chance at happiness, although it is a scary process of facing the very things they run from.

Those who do not have trauma are less likely to recognize their suffering, though they carry everyday wounds that are written off as ordinary, or an inescapable part of the human experience. Most suffering is less obvious than trauma. It shows up in the form of stress, contention, frustration, anger, insecurity, unease, anxiety, fear, procrastination, control, helplessness, guardedness, over-analyzing, self-doubt, poor self-image, lack of confidence, overconfidence, and other related tendencies. Although most therapists would call these struggles normal, the Buddha would call it suffering. He never ranked or categorized suffering because the degree is irrelevant.

Close relationships also tend to create and expose suffering. The most powerful conditioning usually comes from family, even if expectations aren't communicated. Overt or covert pressure to think, feel, or act in certain ways creates the blueprint for getting love and acceptance, but also the blueprint for experiencing shame, guilt, or rejection if you don't measure up. Additionally, many marriages end in divorce, not because the couple is incompatible, but because they trigger deep-seated wounds within each other, all the while thinking the other is to blame.

No matter the source, you can rest assured that every human being accumulates some amount of baggage throughout their lifetime. The only question is whether they've offloaded it or not. One reason few people reach enlightenment is because they do not recognize their suffering, nor do they have a reference point for what is possible. Suffering is synonymous with the human condition, which is why enlightenment exists in the first place, and why it is so alluring and rare.

Identifying your wounds can be very easy or near impossible. If you endured frequent physical abuse from one of your parents during childhood, identifying that wound won't be difficult. Painful memories are probably vivid and close to the surface. Although your experiences have surely left mental, emotional, and possibly even physical scars, the silver lining is you know exactly where to go with your healing.

In other cases, the brain has an uncanny ability to disassociate from painful experiences and bury memories in the subconscious, so much so that you truly can't remember them. Even though a direct link to a painful experience is severed, the emotional remnants come out sideways in the form of self-sabotaging behaviors, unnecessary protections, hypersensitivities, or emotional reactions that are disproportionate to what's currently going on.

In the same way that a doctor uses symptoms to guide them to an underlying condition, triggers are like breadcrumbs that can lead you to your original wounds. Anything that makes you fight, run away, defend, shut down, blame, or control is a surface level reaction to a deeper issue. Reactions are a dead giveaway that you've discovered one of your rocks, even if you don't know its origin yet. Whereas most people blame their circumstances or other people for their feelings, a wise person goes inward to see what is being triggered within.

One strategy to discover your wounds is to notice unconscious behaviors you engage in, but you don't know why. For example, if you get close to your partner and then criticize him or her to create distance, don't accept your behavior as a random personality trait. Your behavior is indicative of an underlying condition, like a fear of rejection that is undoubtedly tied to a much earlier experience or relationship. Working backwards from a negative outcome helps you identify unconscious cycles that are not serving you. Think of it as reverse engineering the steps that got you into a situation you don't fully understand. What behaviors preceded the outcome? What feelings preceded the behaviors? What thoughts preceded the feelings? Where did those thoughts or beliefs originate from?

When you trace it back step by step, you become conscious of an unconscious cycle, which gives you the awareness to explain why you do what you do. The cycles you repeat are what the spiritual community calls karma. These cycles, however painful they are to repeat, contain the very lessons for your liberation. Suffering always shows you the way out of suffering once you understand the mechanics. Another way to unearth unconscious patterns is to do something you don't normally do to see what thoughts and emotions bubble up. For instance, if you normally let people walk over you, stand up for yourself and notice the uncomfortable thoughts and feelings that surface. In reverse, don't do something you normally do, like leaving your house messy for a few days if you compulsively keep it spotless. Instead of trying to make unpleasant feelings go away as quickly as possible, get curious about their roots.

Ask, why do I feel this way? What am I really afraid of? What am I protecting? Where does this fear come from? If I do this or I don't do that, what does it mean about who I am? The idea is to trace your triggers, reactions, and behaviors back to their sources. These are your original wounds.

Original wounds always stem from painful memories that are conscious or unconscious. For example, a five-year-old boy may overhear his parents threatening divorce during an argument and unconsciously try to be the perfect child to keep his parents together. By sacrificing his needs and becoming hyperaware of his parents' moods, he tries to keep things on an even keel.

This perfect child inevitably becomes a perfectionist as an adult, never linking his fear of making mistakes to his childhood fear of being abandoned. An original wound creates a behavior that is linked to an unconscious story, "I have to be perfect, or I will be abandoned."

Think of a woman who is cheated on by a man she loves. When she finds out about the betrayal, her heart is broken by someone she thought she could trust. An association between relationships and pain is cemented, and she may create a story around the disloyalty such as, "I'm not good enough," "all men cheat," or "love isn't safe." A rock gets stuck in the river. She appears to move on from her pain, only for it to get retriggered in future relationships in the form of mistrust, insecurity, or unwarranted jealousy. She may even choose men that will do the same thing without knowing why.

Her relationships become self-fulfilling prophecies because she believes this is what she deserves or that all the good men are taken. Most people are operating from a few unconscious stories that are shaping their entire view of life and relationships. This is how you drag pain from the past into the present. Old wounds create new wounds, thus compounding the pain and reinforcing the need for protection.

Adults often want to process pain in a logical, sophisticated way, like putting the pieces of an intellectual puzzle together so they can explain their pain away. Venting is coping disguised as healing, and it's a surefire way to stay stuck. What is missing is feeling. If pain gets stuck because you suppress it, then pain gets unstuck when you express it. That's healing in a nutshell. Feel the shame. Feel the anger. Feel the betrayal. Whatever it is, feel it and don't hold back. When you allow pain to run its course, it dissipates.

Children know how to do this instinctively. Picture a small child who is crying uncontrollably. They can hardly breathe as they gasp for air in between each sob. Without caring how they look or questioning if they're doing it right, they just feel whatever comes up. There's no need for fancy therapeutic terms, clinical diagnoses, psycho analysis, or even a basic label for the emotion. After crying for as long as it takes, their breathing slows as their body relaxes. They whimper and sigh a few more times until something very ordinary and incredibly profound happens. There is one, final exhale, followed by a sound that can only be described as relief. It is done.

In Buddhism, the word Nirvana refers to the final transcendental state where there is no suffering. However, the literal translation of Nirvana means to blow out. Nirvana is the final exhale where pain is transmuted to peace and feeling is transmuted to healing. You do not think your way out of pain. You feel your way through pain.

Feeling is how your body lets go of the past, but your healing will be incomplete if you do not address the mental stories surrounding your pain. By rewriting, reframing, or reinterpreting painful experiences in a more intentional way, you can consciously choose a narrative that serves you now. This is how your mind makes peace with the past.

For example, if you believe that you were the cause of your parents' divorce, replace that story with the truth. Your parents got divorced because they weren't right for each other. It had nothing to do with you. If everyone in your platoon was killed except for you, reframe your survivor's guilt by remembering that your fallen friends would want you to live your life to the fullest.

Instead of saying that you can't trust anyone, reframe it by saying you can trust the right people. Redefine vulnerability as the courage to be authentic, rather than weakness. Any story that does not serve you must be rewritten. This is not a mantra that you repeat over and over in hopes that one day you'll believe it. The new story must be believable because it is the truth. To get to the truth, however, requires you to increase your awareness, understanding, and maturity surrounding human behavior, both for yourself, and others. Many people are quick to judge others for their behavior. Someone who does good things is a good person. Someone who does bad things is a bad person. In essence, behavior reveals one's character. Therefore, it's an accurate reflection of who someone is.

But is that the full truth? When you reduce a human being to their behavior, judgment is swift and easy. However, behavior never tells the complete story. An enlightened person is much more interested in what causes people to behave the way they do.

Imagine yourself sitting across from a murderer who is covered in graphic, vulgar tattoos from head to toe. He tells you the story of how he brutally beat another man to death over a petty argument. His dark, callous eyes are unsettling. It's clear that he doesn't feel any remorse. You feel nervous and unsafe, so you come to the only conclusion that makes sense. This murderer is evil, and you are nothing like him.

Suppose you learn that this man grew up with parents who were drug addicts. As a small child, he was neglected, filthy, hungry, and unloved. When he was four, he saw his dad shoot his mom, and then turn the gun on himself. He spent the next ten years bouncing from foster home to foster home, enduring regular sexual abuse. After failing out of school, he ended up on the streets as a drug addict before committing murder himself. How do you see this person now? Does his behavior make more sense? Would you be any different had you grown up like that?

Nothing excuses his behavior or insulates him from the consequences of his actions. However, this is not an evil person. Without condoning or condemning, can you see the pain behind his behavior? Underneath his cold, uncaring facade is someone in excruciating pain. Dissociating from his feelings was, and is, his only refuge.

Human behavior is driven more by unhealed wounds, unmet needs, egoic insecurities, and self-protections than by character defects or evil personified. People do not show you who they are, but where they are in relation to their level of awareness and healing, or lack thereof.

Although you will not find the word transmutation in many religious texts, you will recognize its spiritual equivalent, which is forgiveness. Forgiveness is often portrayed as a religious ideal that happens supernaturally. In practical terms, forgiveness is nothing more than a mature understanding that all hurtful behavior, however egregious, is the direct result of unresolved pain. As the cliché goes, "hurt people hurt people."

A man who cheats on his wife isn't a selfish jerk. He doesn't feel like he's good enough, so he looks for validation in the arms of another woman. An alcoholic isn't a person who simply doesn't have the willpower to stop. They're numbing pain. A woman who seems fake isn't shallow. She's inauthentic because she's terrified of being rejected. Your dad didn't hit you because he enjoyed it. He took the pain and anger from his relationship with his father out on you. It doesn't make it right, but it does make it make sense.

Judging behavior is always the path of least resistance. It's easy because it's black and white, but poor behavior is a reflection of pain, not character. Understanding human behavior is never as simple as it appears, nor is forgiveness as complex as you think. If you want to let go of your pain, you must see the pain that drove other people to hurt you. You must also see that it was your own pain that drove you to act in ways that led to your shame, guilt, and regret. This is what it means to be human. More importantly, this is what it means to have grace for being human. Grace must apply to the people you think deserve it the least, including, and especially, yourself. This is how judgment is transmuted into compassion. In the end, it's a choice of what egoic judgments you're willing to let go of to be free.

Rewriting the story surrounding your pain also includes an honest assessment of the good that has come from your pain. Beauty is always born out of ashes when you view it from a higher plane. Who have you become because of your pain? Are you an amazing father because you never wanted your child to feel the pain you experienced because your dad wasn't around? Do you have more empathy because you know the pain of betrayal?

Have you accomplished amazing things because someone didn't believe in your dream, and you wanted to prove them wrong? What did you learn from your divorce other than your ex had all the issues? If you are going to blame, blame fairly. It's not about finding the silver lining or seeing the glass half full. It's about telling the full truth from a vantage point of empowerment instead of victimhood. Some of the most powerful life lessons come from pain, as does exponential spiritual growth. During the healing process, you see it in hindsight. When you're enlightened, you trust it in real time. Then, and only then, can you suffer without suffering.

Having felt your suppressed pain and rewritten the stories about what the past means for you now, the evidence of your healing must also show up in your behavior. This is the external manifestation of your internal shift, or the breaking of destructive patterns and cycles that you've outgrown. Healing should make you cognizant of your negative cycles, giving insight into the functions and protections they have provided you to this point. Understanding your cycles also reveals the beliefs, fears, or feelings you must face to break free.

Your final task is to interrupt the cycle enough times to break it. This is what it means to break one's karma. Sometimes awareness is all that's needed to break a cycle for good. More commonly, it requires intervention at varying stages in the cycle until the fuel runs out. Eradicating a cycle completely always includes breaking it at the level of thoughts, feelings, and behaviors. Intervention at the thought level means learning to stop listening to the voice in your head by practicing redirecting your mind away from thought patterns or old stories that lead to undesirable feelings, behaviors, and outcomes. More on that in the next chapter. At the level of feelings, it means learning to sit with your feelings without needing to change or act on them. If you didn't have a problem feeling difficult emotions, what problem would you really have? At the behavioral level, you simply must make a different choice. Engage with a person or situation in a different way, or don't engage at all. Stop acting out the ego's drama, conflict, or chaos.

Cycles are often broken partially before they are broken completely. For example, sometimes you'll make the right behavioral choice but still deal with the aftermath of the thoughts and feelings linked to it. That's progress. Sometimes you'll still feel a certain way even though you're not feeding the cycle with thoughts anymore. That's progress too.

Continue intervening at all three levels until each component loses its power, to the point where the cycle is extinguished. You are likely to repeat old patterns for a while even after becoming aware of them, so give yourself grace. Healing can shine a spotlight on the suffering, even amplifying it, but that's what makes salvation so sweet.

When it comes to healing, the method is less important than the desire to heal. Traditional therapy, group therapy, trauma workbooks, and healing retreats can be great options for facing your pain. Try different methods until you find one that resonates with you. Alternative modalities like intensive breathwork can put you into an altered state of consciousness, allowing dormant feelings to surface and process.

Additionally, psychedelic healing experiences can be life changing for those who are stuck or cannot seem to get to the root of their suffering. Medicines like psilocybin, MDMA, ketamine, ayahuasca, and others can bypass the analytical mind, neutralize or expose your ego, and heal wounds with surprising precision and accuracy.

Their use should be approached with great respect and caution; however, they can be powerful tools for healing when used properly. Be responsible and relentless in your pursuit of emotional freedom. At a certain point in your healing journey, you'll feel like you've worked through your issues but you'll question whether there is still something lurking in the shadows. This is the point at which your ego will search for a problem that isn't there anymore. Victim mentality is defined as revisiting the scene of an emotional crime again and again. The ego loves being a victim. Healing requires you to revisit the past, but once you've let go of your pain and rewritten the story, don't listen to your ego when it tries to get you to question your progress.

Healing can activate and energize the ego if you're not careful, which is one reason why many people are stuck in a perpetual state of healing. The highs and lows of the healing process can also be addicting, making normal life seem dull in contrast. If the ego looks for a problem and can't find one, it revisits an old wound or creates a new reason to postpone happiness. The ego loves nothing more than to hold on to the narrative that one is never healed, or that you will always carry the pain.

You will carry it as long as you choose to carry it. To be healed is a form of ego death. The old, wounded part of you that used pain as a protection must die. Pain can no longer be your shield or your excuse. That's why the final step in the healing process is making the conscious choice to be done. Whatever you need to heal from, remember that there is someone who has already broken free from it and overcome much worse. You are not the exception to the rule. You are not beyond redemption. You are not broken.

Healing has a universal effect on anyone who has the courage to face their demons. Angry people become kinder. Frantic people become calm. Shy people find their voice. Volatile people become stable. Control freaks learn to go with the flow. Numb people feel again. Those in their self-made prison break free. Once the baggage is offloaded, human beings are inherently good. You are inherently good. You could say that healing reveals the true nature of the soul.

Just like enlightenment, healing is a paradox. You must feel your pain to be free from your pain. You must suffer to end your suffering. Whatever pain is buried or suppressed within you must come out. Whatever darkness in you must be exposed to the light. Whatever false narratives you're holding on to must be confronted by the truth. The only way forward is through. Not over, not under, not around. Through.

CHAPTER FIVE

HOW TO TRANSCEND YOUR EGO

"Your mind is like a bird that has been locked in a cage for many years. It fears liberty. Yet, freedom is its birthright."

-Paramahansa Yogananda

The word transcend means to surpass or go beyond the limits. Spiritual transcendence, then, is when the spirit goes beyond the limits of the ego. The word transcend sounds much gentler than fighting or killing your ego, and rightly so. As much as you may want your ego to disappear or die in spectacular fashion, any resistance towards your ego is counterproductive. Think of your ego as a jujitsu master who knows how to use your moves against you. Throw a punch and the master grabs your wrist, hurling you to the ground. Go for the jugular and you end up in a choke hold. Then, the master helps you up so the fight can continue indefinitely. There's only one way to beat this jujitsu master: Don't get in the octagon. Stop fighting. Stop reacting. Stop resisting. Disengage completely. As with most spiritual concepts, it's one thing to know something intellectually and another to embody the truth. Devout spiritual seekers have often withdrawn from the world in their quest to transcend ego. In spiritual terms, they forsake the world. This is the path of the monk. Stripped of their family, possessions, career, social status, and individuality, they retreat from society. But this act, in and of itself, is meaningless unless it changes their internal world.

That's why monks spend thousands of hours meditating over their lifetime. During meditation, they practice disengaging from their ego. In the early weeks and months, they struggle to break free because the ego predictably clings for control. Instead of fighting back, monks become still again and again; they learn to find inner peace in the safety of stillness.

The real art, however, is sustaining inner peace in everyday life. During non-meditating hours, monks practice being present to avoid falling back into ego. By repeatedly refocusing the mind back to presence, a transcendent state eventually becomes their permanent state. No more ego. They are at one with themselves, everyone, and everything, meaning their peace and happiness are no longer dependent on circumstance. As Jesus said, they have "overcome the world."

There's no denying that monks have an advantage when it comes to transcending the ego. If the voice in their head won't stop talking, they can always just sit in meditation longer. If they can't quiet it that day, there's another eight hours of meditation on the schedule tomorrow. Eventually, the ego has no choice but to yield.

You probably don't have eight hours a day to meditate, nor do you want to. But you can learn from the basic monk strategy. Disengage from the world so you can disengage from your ego. Re-engage with the world, be present, and practice living without your ego. Rinse and repeat. You do not free yourself from your ego by destroying it. Free yourself by going beyond it. Stop identifying with your ego again and again until your ego gets the message: The master is back.

The first step towards transcendence is to learn how to observe your ego instead of being your ego. Spiritual masters have often referred to your true Self as the observer. Simply put, the one who can observe the voice in the head is clearly not the voice. An observer watches from a distance but doesn't get involved. An observer notices what's going on but doesn't judge, analyze, or react.

Your spiritual journey is mostly about learning to live life from your rightful vantage point as the observer. By continuously experiencing yourself as the observer, you will transcend your ego and know that the voice in your head was never you, not because you think it or believe it, but because observing is your natural state of being. All you need is some practice. The price of transcendence is inner stillness, which is why meditation is so prevalent among spiritual seekers. Meditation is like sensory deprivation in the sense that there is nothing to taste, touch, see, or smell—there aren't any distractions from your external world. By closing your eyes and sitting still, you narrow your experience to your inner world.

Subsequently, you are face to face with your ego. What is supposed to be a peaceful experience is often more like torture when you first learn to meditate, in large part because your thoughts and feelings are so pervasive, and because the chaos in your mind is on full display. This creates the feeling that you want to be free from yourself. Of course, you don't want to be free from yourself. You want to be free from the ego that you've mistaken as your Self.

One of the most common misconceptions about meditation is that the goal is to silence the mind or experience an absence of thought. Although that is possible, the goal of meditation is not to control your thoughts. It's to stop letting your thoughts control you. Trying to eradicate the voice in your head is futile in meditation and in everyday life. It would be like asking your heart not to beat or your lungs not to breathe. The mind is designed to think. Divest yourself of any notion that to break free, the voice in your head must stop talking. Instead, make it your goal to observe the voice without reacting to it, which is really a way of saying, "stop listening."

Although you cannot silence the voice through willpower or intimidation, the voice will quiet down over time as you stop listening to it. Sometimes this is a gentle, peaceful process. Other times it can be a brutal, volatile process. The ego is paying attention to whether you're listening or not. When you don't identify with it, the ego is starved of the energy it needs to survive. Like a desperate animal, it may get more aggressive and frantic to find food.

As you transcend, the ego will often push every mental and emotional button to suck you back in. Brace yourself for a barrage of criticism, guilt, shame, fear, anger, or any trigger that worked in the past. You've tempted the devil and he's coming for you. This assault could last for weeks, months, or years, depending on how persistent you are at not taking the bait. Don't give in and don't fight back. Intense egoic reactions can be a good sign that you are on the right track, however unsettling and uncomfortable it may be.

In chapter two, you learned that scientists estimate that you have somewhere between 60,000 and 80,000 thoughts per day. Most of your thoughts are similar to the thoughts you had yesterday. You'll likely have similar thoughts tomorrow. These mental patterns are what neuroscientists call neural pathways or habit loops. In layman's terms, the brain follows a familiar, well-trodden path based on past connections, and out of the billions of potential paths, it repeats what is familiar.

Meditation is a way to observe your mind going down a familiar path, interrupt that involuntary process, and reclaim your power. It's irrelevant whether the thoughts you observe are true or false, positive or negative, meaningful or meaningless, or empowering or disempowering. Do not distinguish one thought from another.

Conceptually, you must go beyond individual thoughts and group every thought into the category of "it's just the mind talking." Once you get to "it's just the mind talking," it's a lot easier to just stop listening. You no longer care what the voice says, which is to disidentify from the mind, or disengage from your ego.

The science behind casual meditation is that brain waves slow down as the mind relaxes. As you go about your normal day, your brain is functioning mostly on a beta brain wave. This is a fast, high frequency wave. Beta is representative of the analytical mind or the voice in your head. Depending on how long you meditate or how proficient you are, the brain slows down into alpha, theta, or even delta waves. These are slower, low frequency brain waves. Delta is the slowest brain wave, typically associated with sleep, yet expert meditators can sometimes stay in delta while maintaining full consciousness.

There is a direct correlation between the speed and frequency of a brain wave and the activity from the voice in your head. The faster the wave, the more it talks. The slower the wave, the less it talks. When you're in alpha, theta, or delta states, the voice talks less frequently or even stops talking for varying amounts of time. The fact that the mind can stop talking at all highlights a significant truth. You exist without having to think.

Time is one factor for getting into these slower brain wave states, but if all you do during meditation is continuously get lost in thought, you'll likely stay in beta. Ironically, meditation can actually reinforce your ego if you spend the entire time identifying with it. That's why you must also observe your thoughts without reacting to them. The moment you realize that you're lost in thought, don't judge or get frustrated. Gently refocus your attention to the present moment.

If you get sucked back down the rabbit hole of thought, and you will, gently refocus on the present moment. This is the recipe for mindfulness, which is the go-to meditation for monks. Sit still, relax, and close your eyes. Each time you realize you're thinking, refocus your attention back to the present moment by observing your breath, sounds you hear, or sensations in the body.

Consider your breath as an example. By noticing the air coming in through your nose or observing your chest as it expands and contracts, you shift out of your thinking mind in order to experience something in real time. You cannot take a breath in the past. You cannot take a breath in the future. You can only breathe now. Essentially, you are getting out of your head to become present. In this state, you are being, not thinking. Frankly, it doesn't matter what you refocus your attention on so long as it interrupts the stream of thought and brings you back to the present moment.

A key distinction is that you are merely observing the present moment, not thinking about it. To understand the difference, try an experiment. After you finish reading this paragraph, close your eyes and listen to every sound you can hear for about a minute. Notice the obvious sounds, but also notice the subtle sounds that have been in the background, yet you were unaware of them. If you hear the sounds without thinking anything, you are present. If you hear a sound and the voice in your head says something like, "that was loud" or "I didn't know the air conditioning was on," you've moved from presence to thinking. The shift from presence to thinking happens so often and so quickly that it feels normal; you're used to the voice narrating everything in your life. Meditation makes you more aware and more sensitive to this shift so you can refocus back on the present moment. For now, close your eyes and listen to sounds you hear. This is the difference between presence and thinking.

Once you learn to observe your thoughts without reacting to them, another profound truth will emerge. Thoughts don't mean anything until you give them meaning. It's only when you latch onto a thought that it has any power over you. A common analogy for meditation is to view your thoughts like passing clouds. Every thought will pass by without affecting you, unless you, the observer, becomes identified with it. Thoughts that you ruminate on are generally the ones making you suffer.

As you get more skilled at observing your thoughts without reacting to them, it will seem as if there is more distance between you and your thoughts. You become like an air traffic controller, directing negative, fear-based thoughts to leave your airspace while allowing thoughts that serve you to land. Once you have that level of control, you are no longer the mind. You are at one with the mind.

Meditation is like learning any new skill, difficult and unnatural at first, but it eventually becomes easy and automatic. Keep it simple. Set aside time to meditate each day and close your eyes. Recognize when you're thinking and gently refocus your attention back to the present. To reach slower brain wave states, try to meditate for a minimum of twenty minutes at a time. Practice longer meditations as often as you can.

If you want to use headphones or lie down to meditate, go for it. Experiment with guided meditations, body scan meditations, mantra meditations, or any kind of meditation that interests you. Don't overthink it or psych yourself out. There's no perfect way to meditate. You are not crazy if your mind is all over the place during meditation. Boredom won't kill you either. If your goal is to free yourself from your ego, there isn't a better practice for building a spiritual foundation.

Whatever sacrifices you make for stillness will come back tenfold in the form of deep inner peace. Like a horse trainer who breaks a wild mustang, if you're patient and stick to the plan, your ego will eventually yield. Whether the voice talks a lot or a little, it won't matter because you'll master observing your ego instead of being your ego.

Before you get too excited, thinking that the only thing standing between you and enlightenment is meditating for about an hour a day, it would be worth asking why monks meditate for many hours each day, and why they meditate every day for decades. There must be a reason or benefit to sacrificing so much time that could otherwise be spent living.

To this point, the premise about meditation is that it slows your brain waves down, helping you move from fast-moving beta waves to slower waves like alpha, theta, and delta. As a result, the voice in your head quiets, providing you respite from your ego. When meditation is done for short periods or practiced inconsistently, this slowing effect proves true. Think of it as descending below the ego in a sense. However, prolonged meditation for several hours each day, sustained over months or years, does the opposite to the brain. In chapter one, you learned that the fastest, most energetic brain wave is called gamma. It's the next (and only) level above your normal operating state, beta.

As a reminder, gamma brainwaves are associated with peak cognitive or physical performance, the integration of high-level information, coherent thinking, and flow states. Gamma is also associated with high levels of altruism, compassion, love, happiness, contentment, spiritual understanding, and a sense of oneness. When the average person takes an EEG test, they may rise into gamma briefly, but it's infrequent and typically registers at the lower range of gamma rather than the upper levels. This is a microcosm of their daily experience. In contrast, when monks and expert meditators take EEG tests, they don't experience brief spikes into gamma—their normal state is gamma. Their brains literally operate at a higher level than the rest of humanity.

Furthermore, when monks are asked to focus on an altruistic feeling during meditation, such as compassion, their gamma levels skyrocket seven to eight hundred percent. They can stimulate or activate higher levels of consciousness on demand. This gamma-based, enlightened state is what the "woo-woo" community calls higher consciousness or higher vibration. Although these terms are unscientific, the descriptions are substantiated by the basic science of gamma brain waves. Think of this state as transcending above the ego. Fear, insecurity, overthinking, and other human foibles only exist at lower levels of consciousness.

This enlightened state is rare and difficult to describe unless you've experienced it for yourself, but the best description would undoubtedly be the end of suffering. Many spiritual seekers get fleeting glimpses of this gamma state but get frustrated that they can't sustain it. Others mistake these glimpses as a sign that they are enlightened, even though their brains are nowhere near the level of transcendence commensurate with monks. There are levels to spirituality, even scientifically speaking. Your experience of reality is completely different based on your level of consciousness. The end of suffering is more than just a set of principles and skills; it's a scientific and spiritual state that is achievable for anyone who has patience, persistence, and an unwavering commitment to stillness.

A few hours of meditation every day for as little as a month can change the brain, and you'll feel it in real time. Whereas the brain was slowing down during the first few weeks of meditation, over time it shifts in the other direction into gamma. Counterintuitively, this faster, more energetic wave doesn't result in the ego talking more. Now you're above the ego, having transcended into feelings of peace, bliss, inspiration, love, and connection to everyone and everything.

As you consistently meditate for longer periods, you'll sense the brain pulsing, swelling, or expanding in a pleasant way, almost like its bathing in the chemicals of peace. The more familiar you become with that state, the easier it is to access and sustain it. Neuroplasticity is the brain's ability to change through growth and organization. While it may seem that neuroplasticity should come from learning or mental exercises, the brain organically knows what to do when the ego and analytical mind get out of the way. There is an intelligence at play that is wiser than the analytical mind, and only by going beyond thinking can you reap the benefits.

If altruism, compassion, love, happiness, contentment, spiritual understanding, and a sense of oneness appeal to you, then you must reprogram your brain to live in gamma. That is the science of transcendence. Stillness is the protocol. Yet, most people will do almost anything to avoid doing the one thing that would change everything: being still.

Now, a spoiler alert. There is no award or trophy for becoming a great meditator. If you have the discipline to meditate for hours but you don't have peace in your life, what's the point? The rest of this chapter will teach you how to apply the skills of meditation to real life so you can live without your ego, regardless of circumstance. You want this transcendent state to become your permanent state.

Luckily, meditation has already shown you the formula. You may have noticed that the end game in meditation is to become present. As unsexy as it may sound, presence is the solution to every one of your problems. If you can engage in all of life without the interference of your ego, you're free. Presence is that powerful.

To transcend your ego, you must accept two inescapable facts. The first fact is that the only time that is real is now. The word present means existing or occurring now. If you are going to be present, then you must exist or occur now. Not yesterday. Not tomorrow. Not five years ago when you went through that nasty divorce that you keep bringing up. Not five years from now when your perfect partner shows up. Not thirty-five years ago when that thing happened to you as a kid. Not even a second into the past or the future. You must exist and occur now.

The truth is that you have never done anything in the past, nor will you ever do anything in the future. When you woke up this morning, did you think, "I'm waking up in the past" or "I'm waking up in the future?" Of course not. You woke up in the present. Are you reading this sentence in the past or the future? Neither, you're reading it in the present. You have never done anything in the past because when it happened, it wasn't the past. It was the present. You can't do anything in the future because once the future arrives, it won't be the future. It will be the present. To grasp this concept, your mind may try to think of time as one present moment stacked one after the other, like a sequence of present moments. In reality, there is no sequence because there is no distinction between one moment and another.

Albert Einstein said it like this, "people like us who believe in physics, know that the distinction between past, present and future is only a stubbornly persistent illusion." At the speed of light, there is no passage of time, which is to say there is no time. It's all just one continuous present moment that is always happening now. This is the meaning of eternity, where there is no beginning or end. You are experiencing eternity right now.

Time is a mind-made creation that the ego uses in two ways. First, the ego uses the past to give itself an identity, a sense of Self. Second, it uses memories from the past to try to predict the future, so it can avoid pain and death. Above all, the ego constantly references the past and the future to maintain a sense of control. Remember, the ego creates an inner world it can control to insulate itself from an outer world it cannot control.

Why does it need to do this? Because it feels out of control in the present moment.

The ego has no idea what will happen. You could have a heart attack right now or get a call that your car was stolen. You could get a promotion that you didn't see coming or win a free cruise from a contest you entered six months ago but forgot about. You just don't know.

If there is one thing the ego hates more than anything, it's not knowing. The ego is so afraid of the present moment that it would rather suffer by reliving the past and fearing the future. If you could stay totally present in your life and your ego didn't intervene, you would never think about the past or the future. They simply wouldn't exist. All that would matter is this moment. You would just be. You would live. When ego is gone, the only thing you can be is present, because the only time that is real is now.

The second inescapable fact you must accept in order to transcend is that there is only one reality that is real. This should be a ridiculous, self-evident statement, but it's not. Most people experience two realities without knowing it. The first reality you experience is life itself. This is what happens in your life, or your real life as it unfolds before you. The second reality you experience is life in your head. This is what you think about your life, which includes your thoughts, judgments, and reactions to life.

The million-dollar question is: which reality is real? Reality itself, or your mind-made reality? Everything going on in your head is merely a reaction to reality, an interpretation of reality. But it's not reality itself. As each life situation unfolds, the ego decides what it means. The ego sorts and categorizes every experience, every present moment, to determine whether it wants to avoid it or hold on.

In the same way that thoughts don't mean anything until you give them meaning, life experiences don't mean anything until you give them meaning. They are inherently neutral until the ego makes a judgment call. What makes an experience bad or negative is resistance. Resistance can be distilled into the phrase, "the reality in here doesn't match the reality out there." In a way, it's a form of disassociating. The ego is saying, "I can't deal with reality, so I'm going inward where I know it's safe."

The problem is this illusion of safety is suffocating you. Again, if you could stay totally present in your life and your ego didn't intervene, there wouldn't be a single experience that would be a problem, death included.

Life is not making you suffer. Living in your head is making you suffer. You've really only got one choice to make. Are you going to continue living in your head or are you going to be present in your life? That's the crux of spirituality. Will you continue to resist reality, or will you fully lean in? Surrender is the spiritual art of giving up control, and the true essence of what it means to have faith. You either trust the present moment and relinquish control, or you don't. You either go back into your shell or experience all that life has to offer.

What if you dismissed the reality in your head altogether? After all, it's not real anyway. What would be left? Your real life, of course. Without judgment, resistance, and protection, it would just be life. You would be free to live it. More importantly, you would be free. Life happens on the other side of surrender. Whatever the present moment brings, don't retreat to your inner reality. Don't look to your ego to tell you how to think or feel about it. Just stay in the experience, no matter what. Feel it. Lean into it. Live it. You already know how.

The same skill you practice in meditation is the same skill you use in real life. Recognize when you're thinking and gently refocus your attention back to the present. The moment you realize you're not present in your life, you are present. The moment you recognize that you're lost in thought, you've regained your objectivity as the observer. To be present is to fully listen to another person without analyzing what they're saying, judging their story, or waiting for your turn to talk. Presence is taking your dog on a walk, and you notice the spring air and the tulips in bloom.

It is crying without holding back when a loved one passes away. To be present is to start that book you've always wanted to write. When the voice says no one will read it, gently refocus your attention back to the next sentence. It is about holding someone who is in pain without trying to fix it, and allowing someone to do the same for you, without listening to your ego when it tells you that you're a burden.

When you are fully present, all of life is beautiful. Living in your head is the only thing making you feel otherwise. Jesus described the state of presence when he said, "Take no thought for the morrow; for the morrow shall take thought for the things unto itself." In plain English, get out of your head, be present, and it will all work out.

There is not a universal timeline for transcending the ego. In principle, the less you fall back into ego, the faster you will transcend. The more time you spend being present, the less time you'll spend in ego. Make presence your North Star. No matter what happens in your life, no matter how much you want to retreat to your inner world, gently disengage from your ego and become present. Your ego will eventually yield.

Scientifically speaking, neural pathways get rewired, and brain patterns change. You'll feel it. Your body will shed years of chemical conditioning as you lean into the very experiences you used to run from. Once you master observing your ego instead of being your ego, a transcendent state will become your permanent state. Have unconditional faith in God. Have unconditional faith in life. For your own sake, surrender, because freedom is your birthright.

CHAPTER SIX

REVEALING YOUR TRUE SELF

"When you stop trying to be someone, you become no one. When you become no one, you become everyone. When you become everyone, you return to your true identity as God. You are in the Father and the Father is in you."

-Anonymous

In the book of Exodus, God appears to Moses in the form of a talking, burning bush. God starts the conversation by introducing himself as the same God that Moses' ancestors believed in. He then tells Moses to take off his shoes because the ground he's standing on is holy. It's only at this point that the gravity of the situation hits Moses—he's talking with God. God tells Moses that his calling is to visit the Egyptian pharaoh and persuade him to voluntarily release thousands of his Israelite slaves. Essentially, it's a suicide mission. On top of that, he's supposed to lead the Israelites out of Egypt to the promised land, even though they have no reason to follow him blindly. Despite Moses' doubts, God assures him that they will accomplish this herculean task together.

During the conversation, Moses realizes that the only way the Israelites will believe or follow him is if they know that the God he's talking to is the same God that they worship. So, Moses does something no human had done before. He asks God what His name is. Perhaps he expected God to respond with a biblical name or a royal title befitting of a king. Instead, the scripture records, "God said unto Moses, I AM THAT I AM. Say unto the children of Israel, I AM hath sent me unto you." As the rest of the story goes, the pharaoh did eventually grant the Israelite slaves their freedom, albeit after some divine coercion. Moses also led the Israelites to the promised land, just like I AM said he would.

In a normal conversation, if someone asked what your name was and you replied, "I am," that person would likely think you were having a stroke because you stopped mid-sentence. "I am" is always followed by another word. I am Sarah. I am smart. I am Canadian. I am Catholic. Yet the omniscient, omnipresent, all-powerful creator of heaven and earth stopped at I AM. Talk about not needing to brag about your resume.

Everything that God is can be summed up in the words I AM. You can be summed up the same way. I AM is the only true identity there is. In the same way that I AM liberated the Israelites from bondage, your personal connection to I AM will liberate you from personal enslavement. Although this chapter will describe the meaning of I AM, the significance can only be experienced firsthand.

The most useful translation of I AM would be: I exist. At the most basic level, that is what you know for sure. You exist. But what is the fundamental nature of your existence? If you are human, then you will cease to exist when you take your last breath. However, you are not only human. You are a human being. The two words can stand alone, human and being, yet they are combined to form one thing. To get to the purest form of your existence then, you must separate that which is human from that which is being.

It's obvious that the human part of you must include your bones, organs, muscles, tissues, and brain, really anything that will perish after your death. This also includes your ego, which is an offshoot of your brain. If you remove your body, brain, and ego from the equation, then the being part of you must be some kind of invisible essence or energy that is not subject to the same physical laws of this reality. Many people equate spirituality with religion, doctrine, prayer, rituals, beliefs, and expressions of devotion. What is often missing is the true essence of spirituality, which is spirit. You can live your entire life believing spiritual truths, even dedicating your life to God, but how can you know spirituality unless you experience your spirit directly and know its nature? I AM is spirit.

Throughout history, the spirit part of you has been called by many names. I AM, being, essence, observer, witness, Self, true Self, higher Self, life-force, and awareness to name a few. Muslims refer to spirit as Ruh. Jews call it Nephesh. Buddhists say Atman. Christians refer to it as the soul.

This inner Self is a core doctrine of most religions and spiritual teachings, though the majesty is often reduced to a belief instead of a knowing. Even scientists and atheists acknowledge the existence of an inner source; they call it consciousness. Regardless, many of the above-mentioned names will be used interchangeably.

As it happens, knowing that you exist is the starting place for understanding who you truly are, for it reveals a core component of your true Self. You are aware that you exist, which means awareness is ground zero for your soul. If you didn't exist, then you wouldn't be aware. If you weren't aware, then you wouldn't exist. You can confidently say that you are a being that is aware. Aside from knowing that you exist, what else are you aware of?

You are aware of everything inside, such as your body, sensations, thoughts, and feelings. You are also aware of everything outside, including physical objects, other people, experiences, and so on. When your awareness gets completely lost in your internal or external world, you lose your vantage point as the awareness. You literally lose yourself in the experience. Said another way, when you get completely lost being human, you've lost sight of your being.

Awareness is defined as knowledge or perception of a situation or fact. Notice that these situations and facts already exist. You just weren't aware of them. This is what it means to become aware. You didn't know, but now you do. What you think of as learning is actually awareness expanding. Science has a beautiful place in society because its core tenet is discovery, however, science is merely reverse engineering an intelligence that already exists.

Knowing how a flower grows is to become aware of a process that occurs without your involvement. In other words, all you ever do is become aware of reality as it already exists. Enlightenment is no different. Everything that enlightenment will teach you was always there, hiding in plain sight. Some people know it. Others don't. True awareness is the difference between intelligence and wisdom.

There are a lot of intelligent, ignorant people. There are also many simple, wise people. Awareness is to know the truth that intellect can only point to. There is no limit to how much your awareness can expand, which is to say there is no limit to how much you can expand. The more your soul becomes aware of, the more it knows and grows.

Another trait of awareness is the ability to concentrate on different things. In the same way that a camera can zoom in or out, you can zoom in or out on anything in your inner or outer world. If you're standing on top of a mountain, you can zoom out to see a broad, panoramic view.

In contrast, you can zoom in as you remove a tiny splinter from your finger while being oblivious to anything else around you. If you analyze your ability to concentrate, you'll find that there are only two places your concentration can go.

First, your concentration will go where it gets distracted. For example, if you're driving and a squirrel runs in front of your car, your concentration is redirected towards the squirrel. Similarly, your concentration goes to your growling stomach when you're hungry. If you feel sad, your concentration is pulled to your feelings. There are an infinite number of things competing for your attention. Second, your concentration can go where you direct it. This is the ability to choose, which is the spiritual principle of intention or agency.

Within the coding of every being is the ability to choose. You have the power to choose which thoughts to entertain, which feelings to feel, which behaviors to engage in, and ultimately, which reality you want to create for yourself. Even if you wanted to defer your ability to choose, you can't because it is an immutable element of your soul.

The natural extension of the ability to choose is the ability to act. If this wasn't the case, what's the point of having a choice? To act, however, always requires energy. Obviously, your physical body allows you to act, but your physical body is human and therefore subject to death. Some other energy must comprise your being then. An entity of some kind must be leaving the body in near-death experiences, out-of-body experiences, and actual death.

If you've ever watched someone pass away, there is an essence that leaves the body as the physical form dies. Think of this essence as a spiritual body or a formless Self that is made of energy rather than matter. It's not much different than invisible energies like sound waves or ultraviolet light. If you think of your physical body as an avatar that only functions with your energy inside, you're close to the truth. Whereas you feel your physical body to know it exists, you sense your spiritual body to know it exists. In practices like meditation and yoga, you become present enough to sense an aliveness, a subtle vibration of energy that exists independent of physical energy derived from food, sleep, motivation, or exercise.

This is chi in Taoism, the spirit of God in Christianity, prana in Hinduism, and chakras in Buddhism. When you are in alignment with your true Self, this inner energy comes alive. During transcendent spiritual experiences, this energy surges, producing the most blissful feelings imaginable.

Jesus described this energy when he said, "thy whole body shall be filled with light." This invisible energy is your soul's signature, aura, or light. As the first law of thermodynamics states, energy cannot be created or destroyed, only transferred. In spiritual terms, your physical body will die but your soul will not.

As you think back on your life, you have probably concentrated your awareness on your experiences, along with your thoughts and feelings about those experiences. Although this is natural and normal, it's a poor strategy for self-discovery. After all, you are not your life. You are aware of your life. You are not your thoughts or feelings. You are aware of your thoughts and feelings. By pointing your camera of awareness at everyone and everything else, you've never asked who is holding the camera.

To experience your true Self, you must do something you've never done before. Turn the camera around. Zoom in directly on your Self. Take a picture of consciousness so to speak. Instead of being aware of everyone and everything, become aware of the one who is aware. A Hindu sage named Ramana Maharshi said, "Your duty is to be and not to be this or that. 'I am that I am' sums up the whole truth. The method is summed up in the words 'Be still'. What does stillness mean? It means destroy yourself. Because any form or shape is the cause for trouble. Give up the notion that 'I am so and so.' All that is required to realize the Self is to be still. What can be easier than that?"

Stillness is defined as the absence of movement or sound. In the same way that you eliminate noise to hear silence, you eliminate distractions to experience stillness. Tuning out distractions from your external world is straightforward. Close your eyes, plug your ears, and don't move. In this way, your external world no longer exists, as it's no longer part of your awareness.

After becoming physically still, your awareness then gets distracted by your ego. It won't take you long to realize that the vast majority of the movement and sound you experience comes from the voice in your head. Ramana Maharshi's advice to destroy yourself is a reference to destroying your false Self. Your ego is distracting you from ever experiencing stillness, which means your ego is concealing your soul. You know you can't destroy your ego, but what if you stopped listening to it for a really long time? What if you sat there until it finally gave up and stopped talking altogether? That's exactly what the Buddha did under the Bodhi tree.

When your ego stops talking, it ceases to exist because it's no longer part of your awareness. Then, and only then, does the movement and sound truly stop.

In the ego's absence, something sacred can finally emerge. Pure, unadulterated stillness. In stillness, there are no objects or people, not even time or space. In this nothingness, there you are, aware that you are aware. For the first time, consciousness is aware of itself. In stillness, there is nothing to do, nor anything to become. You are free, free to just be.

Like a prisoner who is released after years of captivity, you're finally liberated from the heavy chains of your human identity. From a place that is infinitely wiser than intellect, you know that there is no physical form that can constrain you, no name that can define you, and no label that can capture your essence. You just are. You always have been. You always will be. Jesus described this when he said, "be still and know that I am God." You truly are a spiritual being having a human experience. As you bask in the glory of your true identity as a limitless, eternal being, there are only two words that could possibly sum you up: I AM. You laugh as you say it because it seems so obvious. You say it with reverence because it means so much.

The more time you spend in stillness, the starker the contrast you'll see between your ego and your soul. Your ego suffers but your soul is free. In stillness, there is no fear, insecurity, depression, anxiety, judgment, envy, betrayal, or pain. In fact, there is no suffering at all.

It's not that stillness itself is magical. What feels magical is the absence of ego, because ego is the source of all suffering. Spiritual masters have always taught that suffering is an illusion. When the illusion of the ego is exposed in stillness, so too is the illusion of suffering. Simply put, when ego is gone, all suffering stops.

This is why the Buddha defined enlightenment as the end of suffering. Enlightenment is not a supernatural, mystical state of living with the fairies. It is the most normal, natural state there is, the state of no suffering. When the ego's shadow is gone, life is perfectly pleasant. Once you know your soul and its nature, your only duty is to be. You are no longer a human being, for you have reversed the order. You are being human, literally and metaphorically.

Here's what you know about your true Self so far. You exist. You are aware. Your awareness expands as you grow. You can concentrate on different things, and you can choose. You can also act because you are an eternal energy that never dies. Finally, your true Self does not suffer. You do not need to experience the world, read another book, or rely on a prophet or guru to find yourself. Your true Self is always waiting for you in stillness.

To this point, your journey towards self-discovery required you to isolate your Self by separating from everyone and everything that isn't you. Although this serves an important purpose initially, you are clearly part of something much bigger than you. You are one of billions of other souls living on Earth. There is a gigantic natural world all around you. Bigger still, you are a microscopic spec living in a universe that is approximately ninety-three billion light years in diameter, and ever-expanding. You are an infinitesimally small fragment of energy in a colossal energy field that goes on forever.

The question is, are you a separate, isolated being floating through space? Or are you somehow connected to everyone and everything? Your human experience would suggest that there is a clear separation between you and everything around you. Having a body creates a distinct boundary between you and every object in the universe. What about the eternal, energetic world where physical boundaries do not exist?

The next spiritual step is to know the truth of where or what you come from. In the same way that your awareness can get lost in your human experience, your awareness can get completely lost in stillness. Think of it as zooming in closer and closer on your Self until you lose sight of your Self. Few people seek long enough to experience the so-called supernatural and hyperreal. A devout commitment to stillness is the prescription for meeting your maker in this lifetime.

Imagine trying to split open a large stone using only a hammer and a wedge. You don't know whether the stone will crack open the tenth time you strike it or the ten-thousandth time. You just commit to the process of hammering each day without anxiety or anticipation. Day after day, you swing the hammer, never feeling a difference between each blow, never really knowing how much progress you're making. Nevertheless, you trust the process. Sometime later, after one more routine swing of the hammer, the stone suddenly splits in two. Did the stone split in two because of that final blow? Or was it the countless blows that prepared it to crack open?

This is what it means to go beyond. Seek without anxiety or anticipation, regularly surrendering yourself in stillness until one day, when you least expect it, it happens. You go beyond. This is day 49 under the Bodhi tree. The illusion of physical reality splits open and the veil is lifted. Your consciousness leaves your body as you return to a place that is more familiar and real than your earthly home. You enter the world of energy, where the limitations of time and space do not apply. In an instant, your soul is immersed in an energy, a light, that permeates through you to the point where you do not know where your energy begins or ends. You have merged with Source and become one with God. The illusion of separation is gone.

The light is made of a divine love that makes human love feel like a candle trying to compare itself to the sun. It dwarfs the most blissful romantic feelings, the most altruistic human compassion, and even the selfless love for a child. Love is the highest energy frequency there is. There is no end to its depth. There is no end to its capacity. God is not loving. God is love.

In this light, an undeniable truth reverberates through your soul. You are not a microscopic spec in the universe. You are the universe. What you perceive as individual objects in the form of matter are all manifestations of a singular, eternal energy. From the tiniest insect to the largest mammal, from the most primitive life forms to the most advanced, from the Earth to the farthest reaches of the universe, it is all one spiritual energy.

God cannot be reduced to a concept, person, object, or even a deity. God is all of it. God is "I AM THAT I AM." In the state of oneness, you understand exactly what Jesus meant when he said, "I am in the Father and the Father is in me." Without any semblance of arrogance or blasphemy, you know that you are in God and God is in you.

Most religious people accept that they are separate from God during this lifetime, and they'll return to God when they die. Prayer is the next best thing since they cannot be in the presence of God during their sojourn on Earth. If you are exclusively human, then you are merely a physical body here while God is a being in heaven. Therefore, God truly is separate from you. However, Jesus said, "the kingdom of God is within you." If that is true, why don't you know it? Why can't you see it? A better question is, which "you" is he referring to? Your ego or your true Self?

By obscuring your true Self, your ego creates an illusion of separation between you and God. More accurately, ego is the illusion separating you from God. The spiritual teacher, Yogananda, wrote, "self-realization is the knowing in body, mind, and soul, that we are one with the omnipresence of God; that we do not have to pray that it comes to us, that we are not merely near it at all times, but that God's omnipresence is our omnipresence; that we are just as much a part of Him now as we ever will be. All we have to do is improve our knowing." You don't just return to God when you die—you return to God each time you return to your true Self.

Ego is mistaking God as an entity that is beyond you, rather than within you. This world is not your true home. Your human identity is not your true Self. Only those who have experienced God directly know why enlightenment is beyond the mind. You touch something so sacred and magnificent that it defies logic, surpasses imagination, and supersedes belief. It is more real than reality, yet so familiar that your soul knows it is the only truth that exists. You are part of it and it is a part of you. It is all around you and within you at the same time, if time was a real thing. It was right in front of your face, but you couldn't see it. And now, you can't unsee it.

You recognize the wisdom in the Buddha's decision to be a finger pointing to the moon. Nothing he could have told you about the moon would prepare you for what it's like to walk on its surface. The ground is so holy that there aren't any words that can do it justice. So, you follow God's lead and use the only two words that could possibly sum it up. Those who know the truth will get it. Those who don't know the truth will dismiss it. Those who seek the truth will find it. I AM.

CHAPTER SEVEN

FINDING THE BALANCE

"By life's very nature we are compelled to find and maintain balance, or be subject to the symptoms of the lack thereof."
-Wes Fesler

Sir Isaac Newton's third law of motions states that for every action, there is an equal and opposite reaction. To illustrate this, picture a pendulum swinging back and forth. One force swings the ball all the way to the right. Once it reaches the right side, an equal and opposing force swings the ball to the left. The pendulum will swing back and forth on its own, however, it uses and loses a small amount of energy each time it moves. Over time, it swings less and less until the ball gently rests at the bottom. When the pendulum is still, you may conclude that nothing is happening. In a sense you'd be right, but maybe not in the way you think. When the pendulum rests at the bottom, it is at equilibrium, meaning there are still invisible forces at play. The difference is that the forces that were once competing against one another are now in perfect balance. These balanced forces hold the ball suspended, peacefully and effortlessly. This is the spiritual state of oneness. When all of the competing forces within you are in perfect balance and harmony, you become one with yourself, others, and life itself.

The right side of the pendulum represents positive feelings and experiences your ego likes. These are the parts of life you want more of. Think of this as seeking, craving, longing, or wanting to feel a certain way. The Buddha used the word clinging. Clinging highlights the fact that you do not feel the way you want to, otherwise you would not be dissatisfied. For example, trying to be happy reveals that you're not happy, otherwise you would not be trying. You're clinging to the idea of happiness. If you do feel happy but you don't want to lose that feeling, you're still clinging.

Clinging reveals your neediness in the sense that you need someone or something to be a certain way in order to feel comfortable. It's an unconscious admission that your inner state is dependent on your external world. Clinging is like trying to hold the pendulum all the way to the right. It takes effort, tension, and energy to keep it pinned when it naturally wants to swing the other way. It doesn't matter what you're seeking in order to change the way you feel. The problem is that you're seeking it. This is clinging. When you artificially hold the pendulum to the right, you fight gravity. When you only want to experience positive thoughts, feelings, and situations, you fight reality.

The left side of the pendulum represents negative feelings and experiences your ego dislikes. These are the parts of life to be avoided. This impulse to avoid is what the Buddha called resistance. At some level, you are complaining, fighting, denying, detaching, or disassociating from reality as it is. Resisting the negative is like trying to prevent the pendulum from swinging to the left. But to stop it requires you to resist the forces that are pulling it in that direction. When it comes to resistance, it doesn't matter what you're trying to avoid. The problem is that you're trying to avoid it.

The Buddha spoke of clinging and resistance as a subset of a broader category he called desire. Essentially, clinging and resisting are two sides of the same coin. One cannot exist without the other. In your desire to cling to the positive, you're simultaneously resisting the negative. In your desire to resist the negative, you're clinging to the positive. It's a catch twenty-two. A resulting push/pull dynamic emerges that keeps the ego and the body in a perpetual state of bracing for pain while simultaneously longing for peace. What is the result? No peace.

The table is set to resist the negative and cling to the positive, only for both strategies to cause suffering. This is what spiritual masters call duality, or the fight between opposites. Duality is the genesis for the heaviness and burden Jesus referred to, as well as the framework behind the Buddha's teaching that all of life is suffering. In other words, clinging and resisting ruins everything. The ups and downs you experience appear to be caused by external forces in your life. In reality, you only experience opposing forces within yourself.

Most people spend their entire lives bouncing from one side of the pendulum to the other, clinging and resisting without ever knowing there is another way. Buddhists call this other way the middle path. Taoists refer to it as the Tao, which literally translates as "the way." Jesus described the same concept in a different way when he said, "enter ye in at the strait gate: for wide is the gate, and broad is the way that leadeth to destruction, and many there be which go in thereat; because strait is the gate, and narrow is the way, which leadeth unto life, and few there be that find it." To find the middle path, the way, or the strait gate, stop clinging and resisting and it will magically appear.

The Buddha's prescription for clinging was non-attachment. Don't get attached to a particular idea, feeling, person, or life situation. Your initial reaction may be to think that you're not supposed to care about anything. On the contrary, non-attachment is merely an acknowledgement of the fact that nothing is permanent. Feelings come and go. Relationships change. Life situations evolve. Non-attachment can be summed up by the phrase, "change is the only constant."

Allow everything to just be. When it's good, let it be good. When it shifts or changes, let it shift or change. You are not meant to feel up all the time, nor will life always go your way. Learn to be good with all of it and there's nothing to cling to. This is the way that "leadeth unto life," meaning you can enjoy life for what it is rather than what you want it to be. Enjoy the positive half of everything without clinging to it.

The Buddha's solution for resistance was acceptance. Whatever life situation unfolds, accept it. Whatever feelings you feel, accept them. This is not an admission of weakness or defeat. It's an acceptance of reality as it is. The alternative is to resist reality, which is its own form of suffering. Frankly, it's a widely accepted form of delusion. Most people resist the negative because they don't like how it feels, and they fear that if they open Pandora's box they'll never get out. However, the negative never lasts forever either.

If resistance prolongs the negative, acceptance allows it to be. When things are bad, let them be bad. When you need to feel sad or angry, feel sad or angry. Since you're not always meant to be up, it means you're going to feel down. Since life can't always go your way, it means life will seemingly go against you sometimes too. If you're good with all of it, there's nothing to resist. Whereas resistance takes effort, acceptance is effortless. Once you stop resisting the negative, it's no longer negative. It's just a feeling. It's just an experience.

As you practice non-attachment and accept what is, you allow everything to be, including yourself. This is how you free the pendulum to swing where it naturally wants to go. Living this way conserves a tremendous amount of energy that is wasted by trying to control everything, but you'd be forgiven for wondering if this approach exposes you to more volatility. After all, you are going to feel and experience a lot more of what you've been avoiding.

Remember, a pendulum uses and loses energy as it swings back and forth until it eventually comes to rest at the bottom. This is exactly what happens over time as you become comfortable with feeling all emotions and being open to all life experiences. Swing to the negative side without resisting and realize that you're alright. Swing back to the positive side without clinging and realize that you're alright.

You become accustomed to the swings to the point where you react less and less, until eventually, you stop reacting altogether. Emotional volatility in your life stops because the emotional volatility within you stops. At this stage of spiritual mastery, there is no need to segregate life into positive and negative experiences. Everything is the experience, the experience of life.

The British philosopher, Alan Watts, once shared a story that sums up the middle path perfectly. "Once upon a time, there was a Chinese farmer whose horse ran away. That evening all of his neighbors came around to commiserate. They said, 'we are so sorry to hear your horse has run away. This is most unfortunate.' The farmer said, 'maybe'. The next day the horse came back bringing seven wild horses with it, and in the evening, everybody came back and said, 'oh, isn't that lucky? What a great turn of events. You now have eight horses!' The farmer again said, 'maybe'.

The following day his son tried to break one of the horses, and while riding it, he was thrown and broke his leg. The neighbors then said, 'oh dear, that's too bad.' The farmer responded, 'maybe'. The next day, the conscription officers came around to conscript people into the army and they rejected his son because he had a broken leg. Again, all the neighbors came round and said, 'isn't that great!' Again, he said, 'maybe'."

How sure are you that what you perceive as positive is truly positive? Have you ever fallen in love, but that relationship ended in heartbreak? Have you ever started an exciting new job, only to realize it was worse than the one you left? Have you ever achieved a goal that you were sure would make you feel complete, only to realize there was still a void? Sometimes, things that are seemingly positive turn out to be negative.

In reverse, how sure are you that what you perceive as negative is truly negative? Suppose the relationship that ended in heartbreak led you to the person that was perfect for you. What if you learned how to be happy in any circumstance because you lost everything? Can an evil act be the catalyst for spiritual change? Sometimes things that are seemingly negative turn out to be positive.

The story of the Chinese farmer is not about being comfortable with positive or negative, nor is it about being apathetic and indifferent. It's an admission that you don't actually know what is positive or negative because you only see it from a limited perspective and a condensed timeline. Is it possible that everything is working for your good, but you can't see it?

Everything in the universe is set up within a framework of opposites. Positive and negative, light and dark, good and evil, pain and pleasure, north and south, male and female, happiness and sadness, birth and death, just to name a few. The question is, are these opposites in conflict with one another, or are they complementary to one another? Your ego would have you believe that opposites cannot coexist, which is why it clings to the positive half of everything while resisting the other half.

However, this so-called negative half not only exists, but it is necessary that it exists. You cannot know happiness without knowing its opposite, sadness. There is no good without evil, nor evil without good. You do not know peace without conflict, nor conflict without peace. You can't see stars without space, nor space without stars. Males do not exist without females, nor females without males. Not only do opposites exist, but they need to exist. In an enlightened state, you want them to exist. Otherwise, there would be no contrast, experience, or meaning.

In truth, opposing forces are always working in conjunction with one another. So much so that they become one force. Two things literally become one. To grasp this concept, think of a battery. A battery is a singular energy, but technically it is composed of two opposing forces, namely positive and negative charges. Suppose you asked a group of people which energy is good, and which one is bad.

Most people would say that positive energy is good but negative energy is bad. Yet the battery wouldn't exist without the negative energy. It wouldn't exist without the positive energy either. When these two diametrically opposed energies are balanced together, they create a singular energy that is powerful, stable, and useful. This is the meaning of the Chinese yin and yang symbol.

Initially your eyes are drawn to the contrast between the unique design of the white half and black half, but when you view it holistically, you notice that these two opposites are encompassed in a single circle. Two things become one. Also notice that the line between the black and white halves is curved, not straight. This represents the fluidity of opposing energies ebbing and flowing. With a limited perspective, it may appear that one energy is dominating the other. Even so, it always balances out over time. The timeline may not be spread over a week, a year, or even a lifetime. It is measured in eternity.

Without any coercion or force, the universe effortlessly self regulates to maintain equilibrium. This is the architecture of reality, and the model for you to mirror if you want to live in balance and harmony with it. The final component of the yin and yang is that there is a small black dot in the white half and a white dot in the black half. This represents the truth that there is positive in the negative and negative in the positive. Life is always working together for your good whether you know it or not. When you stop clinging to positive feelings and resisting negative feelings, they become one thing: feelings. Stop clinging to positive experiences and resisting negative experiences, and they become one thing: experiences.

Suspend your arbitrary judgements and preconceptions, and you will find that it is you who is creating an internal and external conflict where there doesn't need to be one. To end your suffering, you must align yourself with the rules of reality. Think of it as a paradigm shift from "or" to "and." It's not happiness or sadness. It's happiness and sadness. It's not success or failure. It's success and failure. It's not pain or pleasure. It's pain and pleasure. Are you equally open to both?

Life is going to provide you with experiences that span the full gamut; the pendulum will swing to the extremes and every point in between. Don't act surprised when life is life. Live in harmony with reality as it is, or suffer. Keep pushing and pulling that pendulum ball, or stand on top of it and enjoy the ride. It's your choice. The paradigm shift from "or" to "and" is the spiritual shift from duality to oneness. This is what it means to become one with life.

Of course, this principle of duality also exists within you. Enlightenment is usually associated with light, but no one tells you that the path to enlightenment requires you to make peace with the darkness. Trudging through your internal hell is the right of passage. Evil is often personified as an external source or figure. Interestingly enough, Islam and Christianity both subscribe to the concept of the devil. Shaitan is the Islamic name, Satan the Christian equivalent. The devil is often described as the one who whispers, tempting humanity to choose evil.

Whether the devil is real or symbolic is irrelevant. To reach enlightenment, you must face a truth far more sobering. You cannot be tempted to do something that doesn't appeal to you in some way. In other words, the evil desire is within you. You are merely being triggered by someone or something outside. Blaming an external devil or worldly temptress gives the ego an out, a way to say "he/she made me do it" instead of "I did it." Facing the possibility that you may not be as angelic as you think is ego death, for owning your darkness may represent a confirmation of your fear of not being enough. After all, a good person wouldn't think these thoughts, feel these feelings, or behave in certain ways.

By ignoring your evil desires or pretending they don't exist, you're clinging. By running from them, you're resisting. Of course, the solution is not to give in to every desire you have, but fear of the darkness creates a contradiction within you that must be reconciled. Only by accepting the evil that you are capable of can you make a conscious choice between good and evil—there is no external devil to defeat. Enlightenment is making peace with the devil inside you. Facing this paper tiger will reveal that you are neither good or evil. You are a human being with a propensity for good and evil. Stop clinging to your light while resisting your darkness, and the two competing forces within you will find equilibrium. This is the state of oneness, where you realize that you are already whole, darkness and all.

So far, you've learned the spiritual underpinnings for the middle path. However, the middle path is also very practical. When in doubt about the right way to live, simply locate the midpoint between two extremes. Take money as an example. On one extreme, you have a miser approach, which is that you hoard all of your money and never spend it. This strategy is born out of a fear of not having money. On the opposite extreme, you have a spendthrift approach, which is to spend money in an extravagant, irresponsible way. This, too, creates the fear of not having money because you don't have any. Find the right balance between spending and saving and you've found the middle path. Get too far off the path in either direction and you'll reintroduce some level of suffering. The extremes show you the balance point where there is no tension.

When it comes to physical activity, one extreme is a sedentary lifestyle, where you rarely move. The other extreme is over-exercising, where you risk damaging muscles, joints, or the heart. The midpoint between the two is a healthy, sustainable exercise routine. This is the middle path where the body functions optimally without using extra energy to function or recover. Anything other than the middle path will have consequences. "Wide is the gate, and broad is the way that leadeth to destruction, and many there be which go in thereat."

What about more philosophical concepts like the nihilistic view that nothing matters versus the idea that everything matters? Right in the middle is the truth that some things matter but others do not. Don't take life too seriously but take it seriously enough. Is your life governed by fate or free will? Fate would suggest that your life is determined by outside forces, and therefore you have no control. Unfettered free will means that you're in control of everything. Clearly neither of these extremes are true. The midpoint is that you exercise free will to create the life you want, while accepting that your agency is influenced by other people and forces far beyond your control. It's not fate or free will. It's the balance between fate and free will. In other words, learn to dance with life without stepping on each other's toes. This is how you find the middle path between two extremes.

To close out this chapter, you're going to learn about a spiritual truth that your logical brain may not be able to compute. Nonetheless, it is true. The supernatural elements of enlightenment always supersede conventional wisdom and defy logic initially, but once you experience the truth for yourself, it makes all the sense in the world. The recurring theme of this chapter is that two opposing forces hold each other in perfect balance to become one thing, just like a battery.

Obviously there are more than two things that exist in the universe. In fact, there are too many things to ever name or count. What happens when you combine everything together? Does this same balance and oneness exist at scale and complexity? Or does it descend into chaos and disorder? The best visual to explain the unexplainable is a circle where opposite points are plotted across from one another. In geometry, this is similar to what is known as polar coordinates. (example shown on the next page)

Here's how it works. First, draw a dot at the top of a circle and label it positive. Next, put a dot at the very bottom of the circle and label it negative. Then, draw a line between the two. Right in the center of the circle is the place where the two energies balance to become one energy. Now introduce some complexity. Add a dot on the far left of the circle and label it good. Draw a dot on the far right and label it evil. Again, draw a line between the two. Now there are two lines that intersect in the center of the circle.

Continue plotting opposite points across from each other on the circle and draw a line to connect them. Include any opposite you can think of. Pleasure across from pain, day across from night, rich across from poor, truth across from lies, giving across from receiving, and so forth. As you do this, more and more lines intersect in the center of the circle.

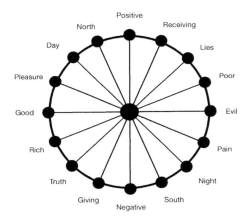

Now imagine countless opposing energies converging and merging at the center point, combining their individual forces together to create an explosion of light. When the explosion goes off, the individual energies become one energy, totally consumed by the light, yet part of the light. Everything is held in perfect balance, so much so that everything merges to become one thing. This all-encompassing explosion of light is the singular truth of enlightenment. This is truth with a capital T. There are no disparate parts; nothing exists in isolation. All opposing energies combine into one universal energy. This is the very fabric of reality. As you'd expect, it is a paradox. Every opposing force in existence appears to be in conflict, yet they all come together to form one thing. To experience everything as one thing is the spiritual phenomenon known as enlightenment.

The only question that remains is whether you will live in opposition to life or learn to balance your energy and agency with it. Clinging and resisting puts you in direct conflict with what is. In truth, the only conflict is within you—life never suffers the imbalance. The middle path is the only path that "leadeth unto life" because it is the only path that matches the nature of reality. The middle path is life itself. Enjoy it when it's good, but don't get attached. Enjoy it when it's bad. Don't resist. Become one with life. Most of all, learn to say maybe.

CHAPTER EIGHT

THE HIGHEST FREQUENCY IS LOVE

"Love is the highest frequency you can vibrate in and the highest state of consciousness. In the pure frequency of love, there is gratitude, creation, happiness, and oneness. Love is all, all is you."

-Anonymous

An ancient Buddhist teaching describes three forms of ego. The first form of ego is thinking you are better than someone else. The second is thinking you are worse than someone else. The third is thinking you are the same as someone else. It's easy to understand how thinking you are better than someone else is ego, but why is it ego to think you are worse? After all, you're putting yourself below someone. Couldn't that be seen as humility in some sense? But the third form of ego is the most perplexing. Thinking you are the same as someone else is the very definition of equality, isn't it? The commonality in thinking you are better, worse, or the same is judgment. Judgment is the operating system of the ego, and it causes tremendous suffering.

Intuitively, you know that judgment is not a good thing, if for no other reason than you don't like how it feels to be judged. It's worse than you think though. In order to judge someone else, there must be someone to judge them against. That someone is always you. The hidden message in this Buddhist teaching is that you cannot judge another person without simultaneously judging yourself.

Jesus said it like this, "judge not, lest ye be judged." Christianity often interprets this verse to mean that if you judge others, God will judge you. The deeper meaning is that when you judge, you are also judging yourself, which reinforces your ego. If you determine that you are better than someone else, the ego feels superior and reinforces itself. If you are worse, the ego feels inferior and reinforces itself. If you are the same, the ego feels comfortable and reinforces itself. All the ego requires is that you continue identifying with it. By constantly judging, even inwardly, the ego has all it needs to survive.

If you're serious about becoming enlightened, the way forward is clear. Just stop judging. In theory, this would be as simple as making a single decision to stop doing something you've probably done for decades. But breaking any bad habit is rarely that easy. A strategy from a true master would help.

The apostle Peter once asked Jesus how many times he should forgive someone who sins against him. Peter threw out the number seven, presumably because he thought that was a reasonable amount of grace to extend. Jesus told him that he should forgive seventy times seven, which comes to four hundred and ninety times.

The question is, what was Peter supposed to do on the four hundred and ninety-first time someone sinned against him? Most Christians understand this exchange to mean that you should forgive as many times as necessary—there is no limit. The world would be a better place if everyone followed this precept, however, Jesus sent Peter on a spiritual journey that would teach him something far more valuable than forgiveness.

What would happen if you forgave everyone who offended, hurt, or wronged you as quickly as possible? What if it didn't matter how big or small the offense was? No matter what, you chose forgiveness. Like practicing any new skill, it would feel difficult at first, maybe even impossible, particularly in cases where someone blatantly hurt you. Nevertheless, if you were committed to mastering forgiveness, you would eventually let one thing go, thus proving it's possible.

Suppose you repeated the process again and again. Each time someone offended or hurt you, you forgave without conditions. Inevitably, you'd get very good at forgiving, to the point where forgiveness would come quickly and easily. Once you mastered forgiveness, you could continue forgiving others indefinitely. Some might say this level of saintliness is the pinnacle of spirituality.

In actuality, you're on the verge of a quantum spiritual leap. Somewhere between the first time you forgive and the four hundred and ninetieth time you forgive, you're going to get bored, and a light bulb will go off in your brain. If you are going to forgive anyway, do you even need to be offended or hurt? Why not short circuit the process and choose to not be offended or hurt? If you did that, what would there be to forgive? Jesus knew that if Peter mastered forgiveness, he would eventually learn the truth for himself: There is nothing to forgive.

The only part of you that is ever offended or hurt is your ego. It's the only part of you that wants to hold someone accountable, demand an apology, or put them in their place. Fairness, justice, or recompense are all to appease your ego's wounded nature. Initially, forgiveness seems like it's about other people. In truth, forgiveness is a mirror that reflects the egoic reactions that are still within you.

You think you're forgiving others out of the goodness of your heart when it was never your place to judge them in the first place. Had you not judged, you wouldn't need to forgive. Practicing forgiveness doesn't teach you how to forgive. It teaches you to stop judging. Then there is nothing to forgive. Will you learn this lesson the first time you forgive or will it take you four hundred and ninety times?

Perhaps your ego is getting defensive right now. "What do you mean there is nothing to forgive? My ex cheated on me. My business partner stole from me. A drunk driver killed my daughter." Most people are willing to extend forgiveness for less egregious offenses, but how much spiritual maturity does that take? Enlightenment isn't for the faint of heart. To attain meta-human spirituality, you have to be willing to go where most people aren't willing to go. In fact, you have to go where even you don't think you can go. Stratospheric spiritual jumps always come from letting go of something that you're not sure that you are capable or willing to let go of.

Where do you draw the line of whether someone deserves forgiveness or not? Where is the line you draw for yourself? Which sins are forgivable, but which ones are not? A good person struggles to define that line. An enlightened person erases that line. The motivation to forgive anything and everything is not about letting another person off the hook. It's for you to offload the burden of your ego. You have to go beyond your righteous judgments to get to pure righteousness.

This level of spiritual transcendence gets much easier when you view human beings and their choices from an eternal perspective. Since this earthly experience is the only reality you know right now, everything seems so important. You could even say life and death. How long is eighty years in the context of eternity? The answer is nothing.

How many of the lessons you've learned stem from pain you have caused others, pain they caused you, or pain you've caused yourself? Where does sin fit in the context of eternity? Sin is the pain that produces spiritual progress. Sometimes you're the perpetrator. Sometimes you're the victim. Either way, you are learning lessons necessary for your eternal growth.

Jesus illustrated this concept in his parable of the prodigal son. As the story goes, a father had two sons, the younger of which asked for his inheritance. After receiving his money, he went to a faraway country where he squandered his inheritance on what the biblical text calls "riotous living." (He blew all his money on prostitutes.) Broke and hungry, he turned to a local for help instead of going home, presumably to avoid the embarrassment, shame, and guilt he felt, as well as the warranted judgment he feared from his father.

After receiving no food from the local, he was so desperate that he decided he would rather confess his sins and become one of his father's servants than starve to death. As he made the long trek back to his family home, the scripture records that while he was still a good distance away, his father saw him, ran to him, and hugged and kissed him. Ready to face a punishment he rightly deserved, the wayward son said to his father, "I have sinned against heaven, and before thee, and am no more worthy to be called thy son: make me as one of thy hired servants."

In a surprising, heart-warming twist, the father said to his servants, "bring forth the best robe, and put it on him; and put a ring on his hand, and shoes on his feet: And bring hither the fatted calf, and kill it; and let us eat, and be merry: For this my son was dead, and is alive again; he was lost, and is found." No punishment, just love. The father knew that his wayward son had already suffered the natural consequences of sin by going through his personal hell. Although his son deserved judgment, he got compassion. Not because the father turned a blind eye, but because judgment is not in the father's nature.

After you have judged yourself more harshly than anyone else, don't you want someone to say, it's ok, you're human. I love you just as you are. Can you accept that getting lost is sometimes the only way you can be found? That people who you perceive to be lost are learning lessons they cannot learn any other way. It may not look like it the moment, or even in your lifetime, but they deserve love, not judgment. The wayward son had to experience sin to discover righteousness.

Although the primary focus in the story is on the wayward son, to the point where it's been dubbed the parable of the prodigal son, it doesn't end there. While the younger brother was living it up with prostitutes, the older brother stayed behind, diligently serving at his father's estate. In fact, he was working in the field when his brother came home, though he didn't know it until he heard music and dancing unexpectedly. After finding out that his brother, the sinner, had returned in shame only to be rewarded, he refused to join the party.

His father came outside, begging his faithful son to celebrate his brothers return. The son replied, "these many years do I serve thee, neither transgressed I at any time thy commandment: and yet thou never gavest me a kid (calf), that I might make merry with my friends: But as soon as this thy son was come, which hath devoured thy living with harlots, thou hast killed for him the fatted calf."

Perhaps you can empathize with the unfairness in this story. After all, the son who had done everything right had to watch his rebellious brother get showered with love. It's a perfectly reasonable argument, at least from the perspective of the ego. The sin is far more difficult to detect thanks to the ego's deception. Having never put a foot wrong, the perfect son felt justified in his judgment, unconsciously using his righteousness to feel superior. His righteousness blinded him to his spiritual hypocrisy, self-righteousness, the likes of which revealed the sinner in him.

Righteousness was his egoic identity, an identity many of the so-called righteous take on to this day. Only by recognizing his own sins of judgement and superiority could the self-righteous son discover pure righteousness. The message: judgment always reveals the sinner in you. In the end, it did not matter which path the sons took, for they both sinned in their own ways. Even so, the father wanted both sons at the party because he knew they were learning the exact lessons they needed. Love is what they deserved. Love is what they got, sins and all.

One of the most passive aggressive, self-righteous viewpoints is thinking that you are not judging someone by trusting that God will punish them for their sins, whether in this life or the next. This is missing the point entirely. The desire for someone to suffer is the very evil you say you abhor. Once you become the kind of person that does not want another person to suffer, you are enlightened.

This is not to spare someone the natural consequences of their actions. Nor does it mean you should compromise your standards, ignore boundaries, or endure disrespect or abuse. It simply means that you do not relish in anyone's suffering—past, present, or future—however justified it seems to your ego. You are not the judge, nor should you get any sadistic satisfaction seeing someone in pain, ever. An enlightened person transcends these petty desires in this lifetime, knowing full well that God mastered this a long time ago.

According to the National Library of Medicine, approximately seventeen percent of the population has had a near-death experience. One of the most universal reports among survivors is having felt a supernormal love that defies description. Some call that love God. Others call it Source. Regardless, most people come back from the other side with an unforgettable sense that they are loved no matter what. A single dose of that kind of love leaves such an indelible impression that they no longer fear life, death, or God.

Contrary to many religious views, most survivors do not experience any judgment in their tour of the afterlife, although many go through a life review of sorts. However, this life review is more like a loving debriefing rather than a trial with eternal repercussions. Is it a coincidence that when pure love is present, there is no room for judgment? The supernatural experience of enlightenment is to touch the proverbial hand of God, which is to know directly that love is the highest energetic frequency there is. Judgment cannot abide its presence.

The closest thing humanity gets to pure love is the love of a child. But even that pales in comparison to what God experiences, and what you are capable of experiencing. Love is often parsed into different categories like romantic love, brotherly love, childlike love, self-love, friendly love, and so on. But the kind of love all human beings long for is what society calls unconditional love. The fact that love must be qualified in this way, or any way, is telling. Few people know what it's like to be loved unconditionally or how to love anyone else unconditionally.

Intuitively, you know that love with conditions attached isn't quite love. But if it isn't love, then what is it? Love with conditions attached is control. Giving love when someone thinks, feels, or behaves the way you want them to, only to withhold love when they don't, is to weaponize love. Therefore, it's not love. Husbands and wives often supposedly love each other in this way, as do parents towards children, friends toward friends, and so on. Many people believe they are giving and receiving love when varying degrees of control are at play. Sometimes control is blatant, conspicuous, and highly manipulative. Other times, control is shrouded in subtle, subliminal tactics that encourage conformity in an imperceptible way to both parties.

Ultimately, conditions reveal your judgments about the way you and other people are supposed to be. This is the criteria you use to determine whether someone is worthy of love, or whether you are worthy of love yourself. In chapter three, you learned that the core fear of the ego is the fear of not being enough, and therefore, not being worthy of love. Judgment reinforces this fear, making you believe that you must be a particular way to be loveable. The ego then projects these same criteria onto others, thus judging someone as worthy or unworthy of love. To the ego, there is no such thing as unconditional love; being human is never enough.

Do you really have to do something or become someone before you are worthy of love? Your ego and exposure to conditional love may suggest that the answer is yes. What if you have intrinsic value for just being you? What if you are lovable, not in spite of your humanity, but because of it? This is the true meaning of self-esteem. You esteem yourself as you are. It's not a hall pass for poor behavior or a license to coast. Rather, it's the ever-present sweet spot between progression and regression.

You're always right where you need to be, if for no other reason than that's where you are. Everything you think, feel, and experience is incredibly human. Being human is enough. You're not supposed to be anything else. Reject the egoic conditions others place on you. More importantly, reject the egoic conditions you place on yourself. Remove judgment from the mix and self-love is all that remains.

This same principle of intrinsic worth applies to every person you meet, saint and sinner alike. Of course, the distinction between saint and sinner is egoic in its own right. Nevertheless, some people are easier to love than others. Again, how much spiritual maturity does it take to love someone who is easy to love? Jesus set a high bar when he said, "love your enemies, bless them that curse you, do good to them that hate you, and pray for them which despitefully use you, and persecute you."

This level of love is only possible if you eradicate judgment from your life. To be more accurate, there is no such thing as levels of love. There is only one love, love without judgment. Either all people have intrinsic worth, or they don't. Be careful what you decide, for you must include yourself in the same camp. Learn to love your enemies and you will know true love for the first time.

As a word of caution, there is a difference between loving without judgment and loving without boundaries. Love has boundaries. Exposing yourself to people or environments that pull you into drama, chaos, or contention is foolish. Sometimes, loving and supporting from a distance is all you can do. Love does not enable, nor does it lose itself by getting entangled in someone else's mess in an unhealthy way. Sometimes love is gentle, cautious, and encouraging. Other times love is tough, direct, even a sobering wake-up call.

A paradoxical strategy to let go of judgment is to stop letting other people's judgments hold you back. Own the fact that your life is your life and no one else's. It's you who has to live it. Choose your life, even if it means exercising your agency in ways that others judge you for. Being true to yourself doesn't need to be a battle fought out of rebellion or defiance. Grace, dignity, and boundaries will suffice. Carving one's own path is often the most difficult path to navigate, for it sometimes involves facing disappointment, disapproval, and potential rejection from those you love.

One of the biggest regrets from people on their deathbed is wishing they had the courage to live the life they wanted to live instead of the life others wanted for them. In other words, they were terrified of judgment. Love yourself enough to live a life that aligns with you. When you know how hard it is to overcome the judgments of others, you'll realize it cuts both ways.

What judgments are you placing on others that make them afraid of disappointing you, risking your disapproval or rejection? Who will be sitting on their deathbed wishing they had the courage to stop worrying about your judgments? The people you love also get to exercise their agency in ways you may not agree with. It's natural to want to protect family and friends from pain, but using your agency to infringe on someone else's agency is rarely an act of love. Whose life is it? Yours or theirs?

This is not to say that you sit idly by as someone self-destructs or is heading towards a cliff that is truly dangerous. Most of life is not that dire, which means many judgments come from your ego thinking it knows what is best for someone else. You deserve the right to lay on your deathbed knowing that you lived your life. Allow others to do the same. Defend and protect the agency of others as vehemently as you defend and protect your own. Anything less is control camouflaged as love. Live and let live. Better yet, love and let live.

It's important to point out that not all judgment is harmful. The wisdom associated with enlightenment comes from experience, intelligence, and the intentional use of agency, i.e., judgment. Wearing a seatbelt while driving is good judgment, as is choosing good friends or using your words carefully. The quality of your life depends on your use of good judgment.

Don't be shy about calling a spade a spade or standing up for what's right. Addiction, violence, hedonism, volatility, contention, and many other life paths are not conducive to peace and happiness for you, or anyone for that matter. You have to judge to make everyday choices and life altering decisions. How else do you course correct, determine what aligns with you, or live with intention?

Judgment crosses the line when it becomes personal. Internal judgment in the form of shame, guilt, and regret are egoic tactics that should be felt briefly but not allowed to linger beyond their usefulness. When you make a mistake, own it, learn from it, and move on. Using poor judgment is often the exact way you develop good judgment. Sometimes you have to touch the hot stove to confirm it's hot, even if someone warns you. That's human.

It also takes judgment to know how to love and help others. Harder still is knowing when to not intervene, insert yourself into another person's process, or circumvent an important lesson that life is meant to teach. One action can be taken from a place of love; that same action can be born out of ego. A particular approach may be exactly what one person needs, and the exact opposite of what someone else needs.

Regardless, you know you've crossed the line if you use shame, guilt, rejection, punishment, condescension, withdrawing, or any other superiority complex justified in the name of love. The more sound your judgment becomes, the more judicious and effective you are in using it. Ironically, it takes very wise judgment to love without judgment.

Enlightenment can be summed up as the journey beyond your ego. It's an ordinary, magical process of understanding and unwinding egoic tactics that aren't serving you, those you love, and those you haven't learned to love yet. Master forgiveness, and you'll get to judgment. Master judgment, and you'll go beyond your ego. Go beyond your ego, and you'll find true love.

To get to the highest energetic frequencies, you must stop spending your time and energy on the lower ones. Trade your resentment for contentment. Swap anger for peace. Exchange justice for mercy. Give up judgment for love. Love is a feeling and an action. It is gentle and gritty, romantic and mundane. Love is a choice and a commitment. It is a way of life and a way of being.

In an enlightened state, you do not give love. You are love. Just when you think you've experienced love in its highest form, you discover more levels—there is no end to its depth. Love is the infinite, ever-expanding energy that created you. It's what you are, who you are, and what you are meant to give.

CHAPTER NINE

SELF-ACUTALIZATION

"Mastering others is strength.
Mastering yourself is true power."

-Lao Tzu

Once a year, a group of Tibetan monks hold a bizarre competition in the Himalayas. Cold, wet sheets are wrapped around the monks as they spend an entire night in near freezing temperatures. If an untrained person were to do this, they would shiver uncontrollably and potentially get hypothermia. Before you think this is merely a contest to see who can endure suffering, the monks' challenge is to dry as many wet sheets as they can before sunrise. The kicker is they have to dry the sheets using only their body heat. Each monk gets into a deep, meditative state by utilizing a technique known as Tummo. Through a combination of breathing exercises and mental visualizations, they can increase their body temperature in their extremities by as much as seventeen degrees. Within minutes, steam starts pouring off the wet sheets. A seasoned monk can dry a cold, wet sheet in about an hour and repeat the process throughout the night. Similar feats like laying on a bed of sharp nails, doing a handstand using only two index fingers, or taking a vow of silence for years show what can be done with mental, emotional, and physical mastery.

In the 1960's, a monk even lit himself on fire to protest the religious persecution against Buddhists in Vietnam. You could debate whether this was an effective strategy, but the most disturbing and impressive part about his demonstration was that he never moved or made a sound as he burned to death. What level of Self-mastery is required to sit peacefully while experiencing excruciating pain and imminent death? Although it would be easy to dismiss these extreme actions as pointless or reckless, it demonstrates how powerful the mind and body can be. Truthfully, feats themselves are not the point. Self-regulation, Self-control, and Self-mastery are the real power. Once you have mastered your internal world, you are primed to master your external world in almost any way you choose.

Math, geography, biology, history, and many other subjects are taught in school, yet the fundamentals of managing your mind and emotions are virtually absent. How much time have you spent learning how your mind truly works? Knowing that your brain sends and receives electrical signals is interesting technical information, but do you understand the nature of thought and how to harness its power? Are your feelings completely dependent on your circumstances or do you have influence and control over the way you feel? If so, where are the limits?

Most people have never considered these questions or taken the time to understand the most fundamental tools a human being has, let alone master them. It's like being given a race car without being taught how to drive. Self-mastery is not mastery of a particular subject or skill. It's mastery of Self. There is nothing else you can do that will impact the quality of your life more than mastering your internal state.

There are at least three inevitable outcomes of Self-mastery. First, deep inner peace becomes the undercurrent of your life, even when things get chaotic outside. Second, you move through life with an ease that makes everything you do feel effortless, even when you are doing the exact same things that once took effort. Third, Self-mastery ultimately leads to Self-actualization, which is the realization of your full potential. The hallmark of mastery is doing something enough times that it becomes automatic. To master your internal state, you must repeatedly practice maintaining your desired inner state in a variety of situations—until it becomes automatic. Before you start, you should identify what emotional target you're after.

Happiness is the state most people say they want, but is happiness a sustainable feeling? Do you really think you will be smiling from ear to ear as you clean your house or go grocery shopping for the thousandth time? It's doubtful that you're going to be happy if you get a call that someone you love has died.

In contrast, inner peace can be felt in all circumstances; tragedy, hardship, and death included. Of course, inner peace does not mean that you don't feel anything other than peace. It means that when you're grieving the loss of your loved one, you have a sense of peace alongside your grief. Experience everything without getting lost in the experience, like sitting in the eye of a hurricane. Obviously it is easier to maintain inner peace in normal circumstances, but we're talking about mastery here. What's the point if it doesn't work in hard times?

The key to understanding inner peace is accepting the fact that you'll never find it in your outer world. It's called inner peace for a reason. It doesn't come from outside you. Inner peace comes from inside you, which means that the way you feel doesn't have to be tied to circumstance. Inner peace is a foreign concept to most people because all they know how to do is react to their external world. In principle, the only difference between an emotionally stable person and a volatile person is the level of reaction to the same stimulus. The difference between an emotionally stable person and an enlightened person is that one is in control on the outside but suffering on the inside. The other is not suffering at all.

Before you learn to maintain inner peace, you must first establish an emotional baseline of what inner peace feels like. There's no magic bullet for this other than learning to be still physically, mentally, and emotionally. Think of it as centering, grounding, or aligning. A calm, peaceful mind and a relaxed, tranquil body is a good reference point. That's why consistent practices like meditation, yoga, or breathwork are so valuable. At first, you may only get fleeting glimpses of inner peace, but as you stick with it your inner domain becomes the safest refuge. The more familiar you become with inner peace, the more you establish an emotional baseline.

Once you know what inner peace feels like and how to find it within yourself, your next challenge is to maintain that state in normal circumstances. As you drive to work and there's traffic, be aware of your internal state. Do you get agitated, antsy, or frustrated? Can you observe yourself drifting from your baseline? If so, you are reacting to your external world in a way that is making you suffer over something you can't control.

Do you want to feel agitated, antsy, or frustrated? If you believe that you have no choice in the way you feel, then your external world is the master. You are beholden to it, like an emotional slave. However, if you value your peace more than your frustration, you'll choose peace. Relax your body, let go of your thoughts, put some music on, and become present.

Don't underestimate the significance of changing the way you feel, even in small situations. It may seem trivial or inconsequential, but it's not. If you can change the way you feel without changing your circumstances, you've found the cheat code. The only question is, how far can you take it? Practice maintaining peace when the stakes are low, like when you're in traffic, getting stressed at work, or when your kids are being difficult. Sometimes you will have to retreat to stillness to recenter. This is not a sign of weakness. You're learning and practicing; failure is always prerequisite for mastery. Maintain inner peace in a few circumstances where you are normally pulled into suffering, and you'll know the true meaning of empowerment.

Inner peace is not a passive state where you accept everything as it is because you're supposed to be alright no matter what. If there is a problem you can fix, fix it. If there is a change that will make your life better, change it. Just don't let your inner state be affected by the problem or the resolution. Be in it and above it at the same time. This is the transition from reaction to intention, from compulsiveness to consciousness.

Enlightenment is the end of suffering, but you must own your role in it. Are you ready to make a conscious choice to not suffer? There is no cavalry or rescue team coming to rearrange the world just to your liking. Defer responsibility for your internal state over to your external world, and it will happily oblige you. In the early stages of spiritual development, it's important that you learn to be comfortable with feeling everything. Then, you're not afraid to feel. In the latter stages of spiritual development, you practice choosing your feelings. Emotional maturity is knowing which emotions to lean into and which ones to let go of. Grieving when your mother passes is sacred. Getting angry when your food order is wrong is a you problem.

After mastering inner peace in everyday situations, the next challenge is to maintain peace when it all goes wrong. Can you still find peace when you get fired unexpectedly, the house burns down, someone betrays you, or you get a life-changing diagnosis? Again, enlightenment is the end of suffering, not the end of most suffering. You've got to push the limits of what you think is possible. How bad can it get out there while still maintaining your peace inside?

Once you can maintain inner peace in any circumstance, you're free. This is the Mt. Everest of spirituality. You have reached the place of no needs, meaning that you do not need anyone or anything to be a certain way. The peaceful, blissful state that everyone is seeking out there, you have found inside.

Enlightenment is the realization that life was never the problem. The problem was always within you. Along your spiritual journey, you practice having fewer and fewer problems with reality until you reach the point where you no longer have problems. Life simply unfolds before your eyes. Jesus said it like this: "Peace I leave with you, my peace I give unto you: not as the world giveth, give I unto you." The world would tell you that you must solve your external problems to find peace, thus reinforcing the egoic cycle of always having a problem that requires a solution. Jesus would teach you to stop having problems. Enlightenment is the discovery that everything you could ever need is, and has always been, inside you.

This is salvation. This is Buddha status. This is Nirvana, where your neediness is gone, and your suffering comes to an end. You do not need money, but you can enjoy money. You do not need friends, but you can enjoy friends. You do not need love, but you can enjoy love. You do not need your life, but you can enjoy your life. When your internal state is no longer dependent on your external world, you have transcended this world.

There's no doubt that if you're committed to going beyond, you will eventually go beyond. However, just because you get to an enlightened state doesn't mean you'll be able to sustain it. Reaching the upper echelons of spiritual progression is difficult, even for the most dedicated souls. Staying there without ever leaving is reserved for those who have mastered spirituality to the point where it's automatic. Enlightenment is no longer what you know or something you have experienced. Enlightenment is what you have become.

Since the beginning of time, human beings have asked, what is the purpose of life? Although this may seem like a philosophical question you should ponder, don't look for the answer in your mind. Let life reflect the answer back to you. Based on everything you've experienced, what does life seem to be telling you about its purpose? Is it to suffer? Is it to be happy? Is life supposed to challenge you so you learn and grow? Is the purpose to love? Ask life any question you like, and the answer is yes. Isn't it obvious? The purpose of life is life.

Enlightenment is the ultimate flow state where you effortlessly engage with life. When your internal world is rock solid, you can enjoy the ebbs and flows of your external world. This is living life to the fullest. Not because you're skydiving, making millions, or sitting on a beach, but because you get to do all of it. Witness the miracle of a new baby coming into the world. Hold the hand of a loved one who is taking their last breath. Start the business you dreamed of and fail miserably. Dance with your friends, fall in love. Argue, worry, apologize and laugh. Cry like a baby and stand tall in the face of adversity. As simple as it sounds, enlightenment is the realization that you're good with all of it. This is what you came for.

How differently would you live if you viewed everything as the point? What risks would you take if you were open to success or failure? How much deeper would you love if you were open to heartbreak? Which fears would you face if feeling fear was a part of the journey? Once you accept that the purpose of life is life itself, you realize that you're playing with house money. You can't lose. You can't do it wrong. Your only job is to experience all of it as it plays out. Don't try to force things to happen or stop them from happening.

Even death is an experience. Death is usually viewed as the death of the body, but death is more than taking your last breath. To die is to shed your attachment to your body, this world, and everyone and everything that is familiar to you. It is the final act of surrender in this reality, a transition everyone must make. Will you approach death with fear or inner peace? Practically speaking, death is nothing more than a transition from one experience to another. As one great adventure ends, a new one begins. Death should motivate you to get the most out of life.

After discovering the inexhaustible source of peace within you, there is no need to look outside for anyone or anything to fill your cup. It progressively fills to the brim and eventually overflows. Life becomes your playground, the canvas upon which you create. Not because you need validation or because it will make you more than you are, but because it's fun. Because you can. This is self-actualization, where you shift from survival to living, from limitations to possibilities. Having mastered yourself, it's time to use your talents, skills, and your very being to fulfill your highest potential.

What do you want to create for yourself and others? What influence do you want to have on the world? Perhaps you'll help others as a massage therapist or an artist who paints portraits that make people smile. Maybe you become a prolific listener, the kind of friend anyone would be lucky to have.

Suppose you become a kindergarten teacher who loves so genuinely that kids remember you forever. Will you keep track of people's birthdays and send a kind note to make them feel special? Perhaps you'll organize meals for a young mother in your neighborhood who just had a baby.

Maybe your visions are grand, like becoming a CEO, running for office, or starting a non-profit that feeds millions of hungry people in a poor country. Your version of Self-actualization won't be the same as anyone else's. It shouldn't be. Comparing your potential to others is unnecessary and egoic. Your path is your path. Your skills are your skills. Your dreams are your dreams. Self-actualization is not about the size or scope of what you can achieve, or even the outcome. It's about being willing to go beyond where you are now to see what's possible.

Viewing Self-actualization as a strenuous process of pushing yourself to the limit would rob you of the joy of the journey. Although Self-actualization will surely require you to stretch past your perceived limitations, seeing what's possible is both scary and exciting. This is the razor's edge between certainty and the unknown. Will you succeed or will you fail? Either outcome is success because you're actually living.

The pressure, stress, and anxiety most people associate with work has nothing to do with work getting done. It's unnecessary suffering mistaken for motivation.

There is a way to accomplish everything without any stress. Lao Tzu wrote in the Tao te Ching, "do nothing and leave nothing undone." Imagine that you have a lot of weeds in your yard that need to be pulled. It's going to take hours. As you start pulling weeds, you feel irritated and overwhelmed, wishing you could be doing anything other than pulling weeds. This is suffering.

Do nothing doesn't literally mean don't do anything. It means focus on what needs to be done, but let go of the irritation and overwhelm. All the weeds will get pulled and, in that way, you'll leave nothing undone. Then there is no suffering in the work.

In your journey to Self-actualization, there will be some weed pulling along the way. Yet the smallest tasks and the largest tasks can all be accomplished by "doing nothing." This is how you maintain inner peace no matter how big of a mountain you are climbing. Decide, act, and go for what you want with passion, but recognize when you're in the flow of life, when you're going against it, and when you might need to be patient until the current shifts.

Be disciplined but not rigid. Be strong but flexible. This is the essence of yoga. As you stretch, there comes a point where you think you've reached your limit. Don't push more. Surrender and let gravity take you that little bit further. Along your journey to Self-actualization, allow other people and the universe to take you that little bit further.

Perhaps the most beautiful part of Self-actualization is that it appears like it's about achieving your potential, and it is. However, reaching your potential will always have a positive impact on the people around you. When you are the best version of yourself, you'll show up as the best spouse, parent, co-worker, and friend. Many people will benefit greatly from your level of Self-mastery and your willingness to be all that you can be. You'll give them inspiration and courage to do the same.

Whether you speak or not, your light will shine. People will want to be around you, even if they don't know why. Of course, there will be those who will be envious, jealous, or critical as they watch you step into your power. That only reveals the stumbling blocks that are still in the way for them to make their own ascent.

When you have more to give, you cannot help but receive more in return. Compensation or credit will not be your motivation, but it will be an inevitable outcome you cannot escape. Jesus said, "give and ye shall receive." At first glance, this seems like nothing more than a transaction, like trading money for a product. But this is the epitome of symbiosis. Even when you give freely of your time, talents, or resources, at minimum you receive the satisfaction of giving. In most cases, you receive gratitude, validation, or compensation in some form.

Do not resist this, for you'll rob others of their desire to show appreciation. Do not downplay your contributions, for others are reflecting back to you what you have become. Don't let it go to your head, which you would never do because you're a master. The more you give, the more you will receive. This is the never-ending, free-flowing exchange of love that comes from Self-actualization.

In truth, you have no idea what you are capable of. That's the whole point of Self-actualization. Lean into the very places you are scared to go. You have dreams for a reason. You'll know you're on the right track when you're thinking, "who am I to do this?" Who are you not to?

Fear is often the lantern illuminating your next step. Maintain your peace, feel the fear, and move forward. Stop caring about the destination or the outcome. Life is the destination and the outcome. Remember, this is what you came for.

CHAPTER TEN

LIVING IN THE LIGHT

"The word enlightenment conjures up the idea of some super-human accomplishment, and the ego likes to keep it that way, but it is simply your natural state of felt oneness with Being."
-Eckhart Tolle

The only thing more mysterious than enlightenment is how it has remained a mystery for so long. There is an unnecessary mystique and incomprehensibility that deters many people from starting their spiritual journey. Even worse, those who are seeking enlightenment are often looking for something that doesn't exist, at least not in the way they think it does. Enlightenment is the most obvious secret there is. Nevertheless, there are no shortcuts to knowing this obvious secret until it becomes obvious to you. Your personal, spiritual journey is the only path that can turn knowledge into knowing. It's tempting to think of your spiritual journey as having a starting point and a finish line that is somewhere in the distance, like a marathon route taking you from one place to another. The spiritual journey is more like a giant circle that starts with you and ultimately leads right back to you. The obvious question is, if you're going in a giant circle only to end up right where you started, why go through the charade?

As paradoxical as it sounds, everything will be exactly the same, yet completely different. People often seek enlightenment in search of the extraordinary. Once they find the extraordinary, they realize that the ordinary is truly what is extraordinary. But you can't know that until you go through the process. It's like falling in love or having your first child. Everyone can tell you what it's like, but you'll only get it once you experience it. There is no other way. You must want to know the truth. It has to eat at you, haunt you, and drive you.

Spirituality is often thought of as a peaceful, reassuring feeling. It is that, but to get to it you have to go through the gauntlet of pain, uncertainty, identity crisis, even questioning reality itself. If you've ever watched a question-and-answer session at an enlightenment retreat, you'll see people in conflict, desperate to figure it out.

Meaningful spiritual transformations disrupt every facet of your life. This is a beautiful, messy process that anyone can do. Real progress is made, not in spite of internal turmoil, but because of it. Few people seek enlightenment or have the fortitude to see it through, but that's exactly why you should go for it. Your life will be better in every way if you do.

Prior to his enlightenment, the Buddha practiced asceticism, which is intense self-denial in the form of extreme fasting. He starved himself for years, believing it would increase his chances of reaching enlightenment. By the time he sat under the Bodhi tree, he was so desperate to know the truth that he vowed not to move until he either died or reached enlightenment.

His resolve was definitely tested considering he made it 48 days before breaking free. He reached enlightenment on day 49, evidenced by the fact that he no longer felt the need to seek. Whatever he experienced that day was more than enough to satisfy him, and completely alter the rest of his life.

When the Buddha emerged from his supernatural state, several of his fellow ascetics were anxiously waiting to see what mind-blowing truths he would reveal. Although the Buddha never personally wrote down what he said to them, many Buddhist texts contain some version of this quote. "I have taken several births and was in vain searching for the creator of the house. But finally, through enlightenment, I have seen the builder of the house. The enlightenment has broken the rafters and walls of the house, and this house cannot be rebuilt again for me. For me, there are no more desires, and no more of birth. I have attained nirvana." This quote captures enlightenment in an eloquent way, giving credence and hope to those who desire this experience for themselves.

In stark contrast, the popular Indian mystic, Sadhguru, once told the same basic story about the Buddha's enlightenment to a large audience. However, he said that the Buddha's first words after enlightenment were far less poetic. According to Sadhguru, the Buddha said to his starving ascetic friends, "Cook something, let's eat. We've been wasting our time."

Half of the audience laughed, thinking it was a joke. The other half missed the significance. Purists ridiculed him online for taking liberties. Detractors even accused him of lying by intentionally misrepresenting the Buddha. People got so hung up on literal interpretations of historical events and texts that they missed his point, thus revealing their unenlightened state. Whether he took liberties or not, Sadhguru's message is no less profound than the Buddha's. In a very literal way, the Buddha created his own suffering by starving himself. All he had to do was eat and his suffering would end.

This is a metaphor for the truth of enlightenment. All suffering is self-created. Since it is self-created, only you can end it. You can have an out-of-body experience, discover past lives, fast until you're on the brink of death, or commune with aliens or the Easter Bunny, but your consciousness is going to come right back to this reality, just like the Buddha's.

Metaphorically, all there is to do is to eat, to enjoy all that it means to be human. This is why the post-enlightenment Buddha is depicted in statues, figurines, and pictures as fat, laughing, and happy. Based on the life he lived after enlightenment, it's perfectly plausible that he could have said, "let's eat." This version of events represents enlightenment just as well as anything supernatural the Buddha may have described.

Without any disrespect, suppose all that really happened on day 49 is that the Buddha got so tired of sitting there that he gave up, having realized he was chasing something that didn't exist. What if, in a fateful twist of irony, the Buddha gave up—and in doing so, he found exactly what he was looking for. What if he reached enlightenment by letting it go? With this perspective of surrender in mind, the Buddha's original quote can be taken a different way.

"Enlightenment has broken the rafters and walls of the house, and this house cannot be rebuilt again for me." Of course, the house he refers to is only symbolic, but his choice of this particular symbol reveals a giant clue about enlightenment. A house is a literal barrier between you and the outside world. The safety and security of its rafters and walls protect you, but a house also confines and imprisons you if you live in fear of what's outside. What you gain in safety, you give up in freedom.

About five hundred years after the Buddha, Jesus also used the analogy of the house. You read about it in chapter three. "And every one that heareth these sayings of mine, and doeth them not, shall be likened unto a foolish man, which built his house upon the sand: and the rain descended, and the floods came, and the winds blew, and beat upon that house; and it fell: and great was the fall of it."

The house is a symbol for your ego, your mental walls and emotional protections. Ego is the imaginary, safe place inside where you think that by worrying, fearing, and protecting yourself from reality, it will actually work. When the weather is good and life is easy, the rafters and walls will stand. However, when the rain pours, the wind blows, and the floods come—when reality gets too real, the house gets destroyed.

Even though protection is only an illusion, you cling to it because you're afraid. Each time your ego is incapable of protecting you, you rebuild the rafters and walls thinking this will be the time the house can withstand the storm. The Buddha said, "this house cannot be rebuilt again for me," implying that it had been torn down and rebuilt before. How many times did he separate from his ego only to get sucked back in when reality was too much to bear? How many times did he let his walls and protections down only to trade freedom for the illusion of safety once more?

One phrase in the Buddha's quote reveals the secret of how he reached enlightenment. "For me, there are no more desires." There it is. All you must do to become enlightened is get rid of your desires. Most religions subscribe to this concept by encouraging restraint or discipline with one's desires for power, money, pleasure, and so on. In an attempt to eradicate desire completely, some spiritual seekers give up their possessions, maintain a lowly social status, and abstain from food, intimacy, relationships, and other natural human desires.

The Buddha made all these sacrifices prior to enlightenment, yet enlightenment eluded him. After enlightenment, he abandoned all extremes, choosing moderation in the form of the middle path. In other words, the Buddha did not drastically curb his human desires and live a disciplined life of self-denial as an enlightened being. Eradicating your desires must mean something entirely different then. The answer evades even the most stalwart disciples because the truth is so simple that its profoundness is overlooked.

What if you gave up all your desires for control, protection, and safety, trusting that God, the universe, and life know exactly what they are doing? What if you surrendered your desire for reality to be the way you want it be, and instead, embraced reality as it is? What if you gave up your desire to cling and resist, and you were completely open to experience all that it means to be human? What if, in a fateful twist of irony, you gave up—and in doing so, you found exactly what you were looking for.

Jesus said it like this: "For he that will save his life shall lose it; and whosoever will lose his life for my sake shall find it." Hold on to the imaginary life you want, and you will miss the life you have. Give up the life you want, and you will find the true purpose of your life, which is to live it. By abandoning your desires, which are your preferences, judgments, reactions, and grievances with life, you will find real life. You can cling. You can resist. But remember that the nature of reality is not going to change. Something about the way you think, feel, and interact with reality must change if you want to break free.

To become enlightened, you must make a fundamental decision about your approach to life. Are you going to brace yourself from life? Or are you going to embrace life? Are you all in? Or are you still afraid to be free? On day 49, the Buddha's ego died one last time, never to be reborn again. His house could not be rebuilt because the he realized he was the builder. When he no longer needed to protect himself from reality, he no longer needed his ego. His ego wanted safety, but his soul wanted freedom more. He joined the club of spiritual masters, those rare souls who fully embrace the human experience, suffering and all. On day 49, the Buddha finally understood the paradox of enlightenment. By giving up his desire to not suffer, he ended his suffering.

Embracing life is easy when things are good. Anyone can do that. Mastery is to embrace reality no matter the pain, even in death. As Jesus hung on the cross with nails in his feet and hands, painfully anticipating death, he showed humanity what is possible. He prayed, "Father, if thou be willing, remove this cup from me: nevertheless not my will, but thine, be done."

His desire for the pain to end was trumped only by his desire to experience everything his human journey had to offer, even pain and death. An unjust, painful death was his reality, yet he did not resist his fate. He wanted to live it until he took his very last breath. In the years before his experience in the garden of Gethsemane, his unfair trial, and barbaric crucifixion, he leaned into life. He practiced surrendering enough in life that he could surrender equally in death. Jesus understood giving up desire at a far greater level than most people can fathom, thus cementing himself as an ideal that humanity could strive toward.

You can know the truth about God, the nature of reality, and the purpose of life through a mystical experience. Ultimately, it's going to lead you right back to this experience. You're here, so be here. And if you're going to be here, enjoy everything that this experience has to offer. Enlightenment is the realization that there is no such thing as a spiritual experience. You're not being spiritual when you go to church, meditate, or rocket to the moon during a transcendental experience. Life is the spiritual experience. The present moment is the spiritual experience. The present moment is enlightenment. Until the present moment is enough for you, nothing else will be.

The Buddha understood the impermanence and fleeting nature of all experiences, the supernatural included. One experience is no more the truth than another. Enlightenment is a state for this realm—this reality, not for you to go gallivanting in another one. You will reach enlightenment much faster if you rid yourself of the idea that a supernatural experience is going to change everything. It's one possibility during your human experience, nothing more.

Enlightenment is the most normal, down-to-earth state there is. It's really a counterintuitive strategy of not trying to be anything other than human. At the core, that is what's wrong with humanity. Most people spend their entire lives trying to avoid being human. It's why people numb and try to blend in. It's why they keep secrets and feel shame, guilt, and remorse. It's why they try to stand out, impress others, and prove their worth. Humanity is desperate to not be human.

One reason why being human seems so hard is because the ego is terrified that being human is not enough. That's why it hides or compensates. Your choice in this life is to conform to your ego or transcend it. Embracing everything that it means to be human is the way out. Another reason why being human is so hard is because it's foreign to your soul. Consciousness is limitless and unrestricted, free from the constraints of a physical body and the material world. This reality is dense, heavy, and restrictive. Enlightenment is to finally gel with your avatar, having accepted all its capabilities and limitations.

Being comfortable with being human is so rare that it's described as the end of suffering. It's given a fancy name like enlightenment. People assume you have a special power, that you know something they don't. They perceive something about you that they want for themselves. Of course, this is all true, but it won't feel that way to you. You simply know who you truly are and how to suffer without suffering. You know the nature of reality and how to live in lockstep with it. You get the most out of your human experience because you willingly feel and experience things others avoid. Turns out that when you make peace with being completely human, you become superhuman.

Spiritual teachers often say that when you are enlightened, you become transparent. The word transparent means allowing light to pass through. That's all enlightenment is. Allowing the light to pass through. Remember, darkness is merely the absence of light. Your ego is the darkness that is blocking the light of your consciousness, but only when you lose sight of your true Self. All you have to do is let the light in. It's already there. It's always there. Don't blame your ego. Don't fight it. Many spiritual seekers have naively thought that they will reach enlightenment when they don't have an ego anymore.

Trying to rid yourself of your ego is the most egoic thing you can do, but also a predictable step towards accepting the fact that you can't get rid of it. There's nothing to get rid of. In the same way that ghosts are only real for those who believe in them, so too is ego real for those who misidentify the voice in their head as who they are. In the same way that you can't kill a ghost because it's already dead, you can't get rid of an ego that doesn't exist.

Think of the spiritual journey as having three phases. The first phase is unconsciousness, which is where you completely identify with your mind. There is only one version of you, but you have mistaken the voice in your head as who you are. This is the predominate state for most of humanity, even religious people who find spirituality at the level of belief. Beliefs can create an ironclad attachment to the mind, making the person miss higher truths and principles that cannot be discovered without letting go of ego-based pseudo-certainty.

A man who devoted his entire life to God once came to the Buddha and asked, "Is there a God?" The Buddha said, "No." That same day, an atheist approached the Buddha and asked, "Is there a God?" The Buddha said, "Yes." Confused, the Buddha's disciples couldn't understand why he gave conflicting answers, but his reply was right for each man. The believer needed to let go of his attachment to belief to discover the truth. The nonbeliever needed to let go of his attachment to non-belief to discover the truth. In either case, both men identified with the mind, which is spiritual unconsciousness. Only by abandoning their attachments to certainty would enlightenment become possible. From an enlightened vantage point, unconsciousness is easy to spot in others, partially because it is born from ignorance or rigidity, but also because all enlightened people recognize and empathize with unconsciousness because they were once unconscious too.

The second phase is semi-consciousness, an in-between state where you have awakened to the true essence of your being, but you are painfully aware of your ego. The clear indicator that you are in this phase is that there are two versions of you, you and your ego. You experience moments or extended periods of presence, and therefore no suffering, but you still fall back into the ego's control before realizing you went unconscious again. The house is destroyed and rebuilt. Ego death leads to rebirth.

In this phase, you may long for a return to unconsciousness because ignorance was bliss or the illusion of certainty was reassuring. At the same time, a part of you knows that there's no going back; semi-consciousness creates the frustration and suffering needed to find the way out. This is the most difficult phase to transcend. Frankly, it's the only phase to transcend. The third and final phase is full consciousness, where you have spent enough time grounded in awareness to no longer get pulled back into ego. Leaning into every experience is your only desire. You return to a singular Self, only this time you identify exclusively with your being. Ego appears to disappear, when in reality it was never real in the first place.

When you mistake the voice in your head as who you are, ego is real. However, once you know that the voice in your head is nothing more than your mind talking, it's not ego anymore. It's just the mind talking. From there, it's a simple question of whether you control your mind or your mind controls you. When you are conscious, your mind becomes your co-creator instead of your saboteur.

You are the builder of the house, the creator of this second-self known as ego. Ego was your imaginary protector, your mental and emotional shield from truths about yourself that you were not ready to accept, a cushion softening reality as it is. Ego was something you could blame when you behaved in ways you didn't understand, a way to defer responsibility for your peace and happiness. Like a child who outgrows the need for an imaginary friend, you spiritually outgrow the need for your imaginary protector. All the ego needs is for the light of your consciousness to pass through to expose it for the illusion that it is. Being transparent means that you allow all thoughts, feelings, and experiences to pass through you. You become empty in a sense, no longer accumulating mental, emotional, and physical baggage. The past no longer defines you or holds you back. The future is no longer the salvation that you think will make you whole. When you are present, your only job is to allow reality to pass through you without it getting stuck. There is no magic involved.

When you have a choice, choose to not suffer. Face your challenges, change your circumstances, create the life you want. But when you don't have a choice—when reality is unchangeable—choose to not suffer. Continue living the experience without fear or reservation. With your guidance and persistence, even the mind can learn to stop clinging and resisting.

In its most basic form, enlightenment is to know yourself as you are, other people as they are, and reality as it is. Knowing these truths will make people think you are crazy, prophetic, or both. Think of an unenlightened state as wearing a pair of slightly distorted glasses. When you look in the mirror, these glasses show your human form in exquisite detail, perhaps too much detail. Yet these glasses cannot pick up the light frequency of your soul. When you see others, you also see their humanity up close. Again, their soul's frequency is invisible to you. As you view the world and your life experiences through these glasses, there is a cloudy haze, but that's how everyone else sees the world too. Imagine taking these glasses off and suddenly you see energetic light frequencies and vibrant colors that you've never seen before. Light is in everyone and everything. It was always there, right in front of your face. Nothing out there changed. You're just seeing everything clearly for the first time.

Spiritual masters seem like wizards because they have taken off the distorted glasses of their ego. They know the obvious secret. They do not possess supernatural powers or psychic abilities. They wanted to know. They had to know. What is the obvious secret? If a spiritual master was sitting next to you right now, they might say, "can you see it? It's right here, right now. It's all around you. It's in you." Your mind will start to wonder, "what are they talking about?"

Silence your mind and simultaneously notice what you are aware of, and who is aware of it. With your distorted glasses on, this simple exercise would make you think that the spiritual master is delusional. With your glasses off, you'll know the obvious secret. It's right in front of your nose. It's just out of reach for the mind to comprehend, yet it is the truth, plain as day. Upon discovering the truth, many spiritual seekers begin to laugh, partly because of how incredibly simple it is. In that same laugh, there is an unspeakable reverence for how simply incredible it is. Enlightenment is not the accumulation of spiritual truths to the point where you have everything figured out. Enlightenment is the realization that there is nothing to figure out.

As you make your way around the circular path of spirituality, you'll be tempted to think that you reached enlightenment through meditation, yoga, scriptures, fasting, gurus, or by finding God. In other words, practices and beliefs are what got you there. The Buddha compared practices and beliefs to a raft that is meant to get you from one shore to the other. Once you reach the other side, the raft has served its purpose, and it should be left behind. Honor all the beliefs, practices, and people who helped you reach the other shore, but recognize when you have gone from belief to knowing, from practices to being, and from dependence to self-assurance. Spiritually speaking, letting go of the raft is the last step towards standing on your own two feet. You should not feel guilt or fear in letting it go.

Remember, the Buddha said, "I am a finger pointing to the moon. Don't look at me. Look at the moon." Enlightenment is knowing that you do not need your version of the Buddha anymore, for you too have become the awakened one. He would be happy to know that he provided you with the raft.

In the end, enlightenment is not a thing. Rather, enlightenment is nothing. It is the silence that serves as the backdrop for music, the sound of a human voice, and a wave crashing on the beach. It's the 99.9% empty space in an atom, and the same empty space that serves as the stage for reality as you know it. It is the stillness from which all thought, creativity, and expression can be observed. Enlightenment is the nothingness that makes something possible.

Enlightenment is also everything. It is the sunlight that feeds plants, which in turn produce the oxygen you breathe. It is sorrow that makes joy that much sweeter, and the beauty of every kind of tear that falls down your cheek. It's a mother nursing her baby, and that same baby who will one day nurse her mother in old age. It's individuality that makes oneness possible, and oneness that makes individuality possible. Enlightenment is the singular, eternal energy that is always connected, only masking its oneness through the veil of physical form. It is the universe. It is God. It is you.

Ironically, when you know nothing, you know everything. In a practical sense, when you stop pretending that you know everything, you can be taught. In a spiritual sense, when you stop trying to figure everything out, the answers become self-evident. You've simply been too busy trying to understand enlightenment to experience it.

Jesus said, "seek and ye shall find." However, he did not tell you what to seek or what you would find. Spoon feeding you the answer would make you think that you understand when you have no clue. It would ruin the simplicity and majesty of what you will discover along the way. "Seek and ye shall find" is a promise you can count on. Eventually you will get clear about what you're seeking, and it's only a matter of time before you'll find it. You'll know it. You'll know it because you won't feel the need to seek anymore. When you are enlightened, you won't walk around telling people that you're enlightened. Not because you're humble or unassuming, but because you'll realize that enlightenment is only a concept, another egoic idea of what a human being can become. Nevertheless, the illusion is worth the pursuit, for it becomes your reality. Enlightenment truly is the ultimate paradox. Once you realize enlightenment is not real, you've reached it. Your circular journey is complete. You're right back to yourself, exactly the same, yet completely different.

What will you do when you go beyond enlightenment? You'll live and you'll love. You'll be and you'll do. Life is the great adventure and the infinite possibility. Your spiritual journey appears like it's a progression from darkness towards the light. Of course, spiritual progress is real, but it's not actually progression. It's only a realization, the realization that you are already in the light. In fact, you have always been in the light. There's no other place you can be.

Light is energy, unbound by physical constraints in the same way that your consciousness is infinite and eternal. Spirituality is nothing more than a remembering, a realization, an enlightenment that you are always in the light, and the light is always in you. What does that mean? You are already enlightened. You're just in varying stages of waking up to it, becoming comfortable with it, and owning it as your true nature.

You are the state within light.

STATE WITHIN LIGHT

ACKNOWLEDGMENTS

My spiritual journey and the completion of this book would not have been possible without the help of amazing family and friends.

To my wife, Rhiannon: You are my best friend, my love, and my spiritual companion. I love that I get to do life with you. Our spiritual journeys are forever intertwined, and I am all the better for it.

To my parents, Michael and Kimberly Crossley: Without you, I would not be who I am today. Your love, support, and deep commitment to spirituality gave me a foundation that I am grateful for.

To my friend, Cory Morin: Thank you for being the first to read and edit each chapter. Your insight, feedback, and encouragement are embedded in every page.

AUTHOR'S BOOK RECOMMENDATIONS

"The Surrender Experiment" by Michael Singer

"Claim Your Power" by Mastin Kipp

"The Power of Now" by Eckhart Tolle

"The Alchemist" by Paulo Coelho

"Tao Te Ching" by Lao Tzu

"You Are The Placebo" by Dr. Joe Dispenza

"The Mountain is You" by Brianna West

STATE WITHIN LIGHT

Printed in Dunstable, United Kingdom